EAT JAPAN

The complete companion to Japan's cuisine and food culture

CONTENTS

Right: A chef prepares
futo-maki (thick sushi rolls)
Next page: Diners survey the
menu at a Tokyo restaurant

FOREWORD

Washoku (Japanese food) is refined and delicate, strongly connected to nature and highly seasonal. Its freshness is one of the defining hallmarks of the cuisine, where fresh fish and seafood are often eaten raw, and many vegetables are eaten in as natural a state as possible. Japan has earnt a reputation around the globe for producing healthy food.

There are five principles of *washoku*. It's suggested that every meal should include *goshiki* (five colours): red, yellow, green, black and white. It's thought that by including a mix of colourful foods, you are creating a balance of vitamins and minerals. The second principle suggests the meal should incorporate a balance of flavours – salty, sour, sweet, bitter and spicy. A third principle refers to the food preparation, in that a variety of cooking methods should be used, whether that be simmering and broiling or steaming, in order to limit the amount of salt, oil and sugar required.

The fourth principle, called *go kan mo* (or the Five Outlooks) deals with basic rules concerning how food is eaten and enjoyed, and is strongly linked to Buddhism. It encourages eaters to respect the efforts taken to cultivate and prepare the food, and to eat not just for nourishment but also for spiritual well-being. And finally, the fifth principle instructs people to be mindful of all of your senses while eating. It's believed that food should be devoured with all five senses: not just smell, taste and sight, but also touch (the texture of ingredients, the smooth warmth of bamboo chopsticks), and even sound (a high-end ryotei is oddly quiet, the better to appreciate the experience of eating). Any Japanese meal – from simple home-cooked fare to the most structured, formal *kaiseki* – aims to blend each of these elements for balance and nutrition.

Much like the Japanese character, Japanese food has been shaped by the nation's history. The rise of Buddhism in Japan, over a millennium ago, significantly influenced the Japanese diet. Emperors banned the eating of meat, and Japanese staples such as sushi and sashimi became a dominant part of the cuisine. After decades of isolation, Japan's food began to reshape itself under Western influence after Commodore Perry sailed into Edo Bay in 1853, and the Westernisation of its cuisine became apparent after the Americans post-WWII and the popularity of *yoshoku* (Western-style food) surged.

Today, Japanese cuisine is as modern and groundbreaking as it is traditional and rooted in history. Sushi, tea, soba and sake masters continue to perfect their art, handed down generation to generation, while gastronomic French restaurants, inventive modern *kaiseki* and specialist coffee roasters breathe new life into the culture of Japanese food and drink.

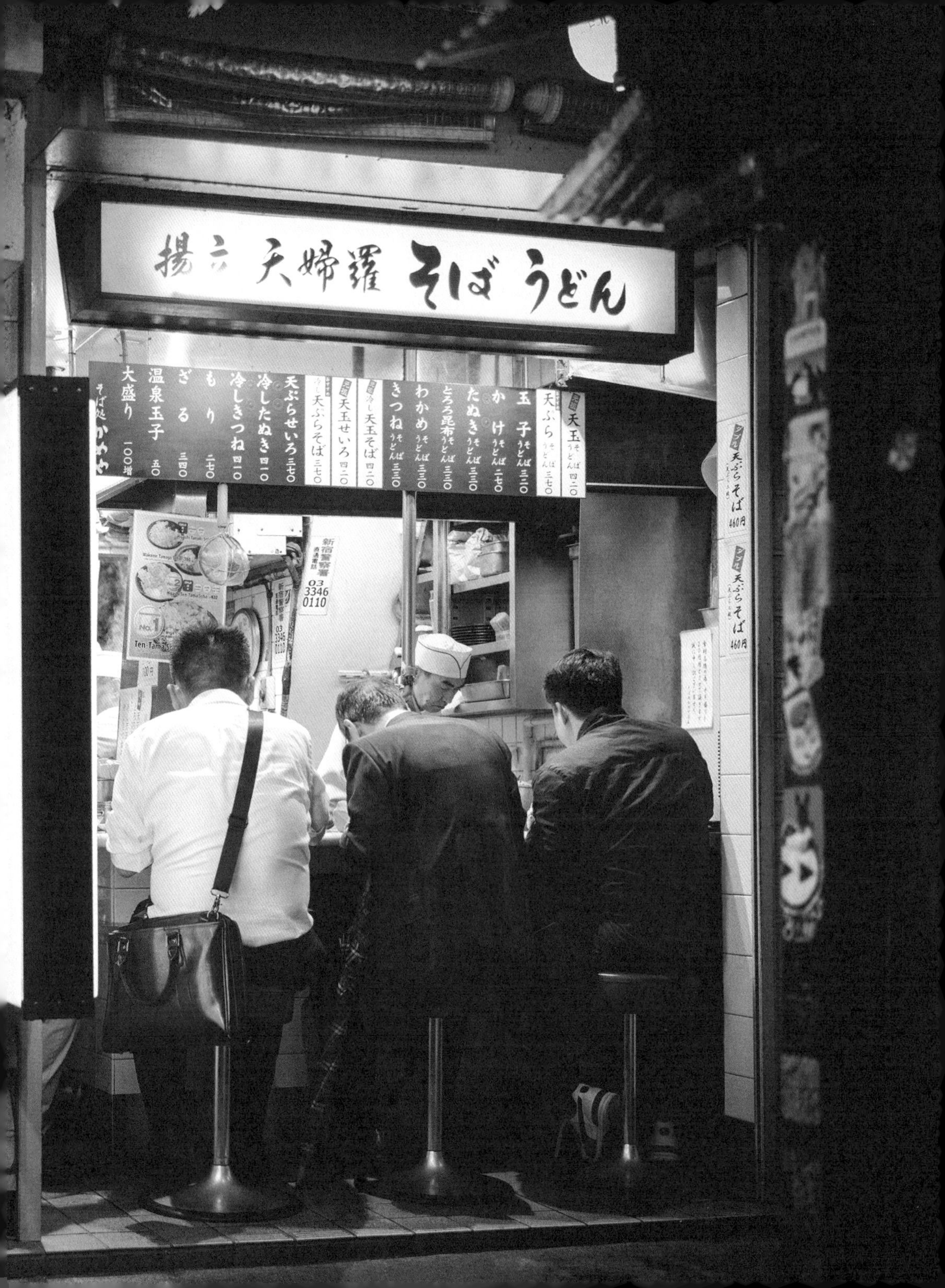
揚立 天婦羅 そば うどん
天ぷらそば 460円
新宿警察署
03 3346 0110

HISTORY & CULTURE

As visitors to Japan quickly discover, the people here are absolutely obsessed with food. You'll find that every island and region of Japan has its own *meibutsu* (local speciality) that is a point of pride. Food permeates every walk of life, and figures large in even the most casual of conversations. The seemingly routine everyday phrase, *'Gohan tabe ni ikko!'* ('Let's go eat together') is no mere suggestion akin to *'Let's grab a burger'*. It's an invitation to commune over food, to bond in a primal act of mutual celebration, to reinforce group identities, or welcome outsiders into the fold over a beer.

Japanese cuisine is known as *washoku*, literally meaning 'harmony of food'. *Washoku* encompasses the traditional dishes and recipes of Japan – food that nourishes the soul. It offers something for everyone. There's variety, colour, texture and subtlety. There's the exquisite marriage of form and function, the immaculate presentation. From deep-fried *age-dashi-nasu* eggplants to *zosui* rice soup, from the succulent fresh salmon of Hokkaido to the fiery, fermented bean curd of Okinawa, from the comforting carbohydrates of a loaded bowl of ramen to the refined and elegant Kyoto high-class *kaiseki* (Japanese haute-cuisine) – it's endlessly variable and consistently tempting. All of this hinges on the proper skills and knowledge of Japanese cooking that has been handed down over generations and is why *washoku* was added to Unesco's Intangible Cultural Heritage list in 2013.

At its best, Japanese food is highly seasonal, drawing on fresh local ingredients coaxed into goodness with a light touch. Rice is central; the word for 'rice' and for 'meal' are the same: *gohan*. Miso soup and pickled vegetables, *tsukemono*, often round out the meal. But from there Japanese food can vary tremendously; it can be light and delicate (as it is often thought to be) but it can also be hearty and robust. Low fat, packed with minerals and vitamins, Japanese cuisine is known to be one of the healthiest cuisines in the world, and it is considered a major factor in Japan's remarkable longevity rates. The Okinawans, with their diet heavily dependent on *konbu*

© Jonathan Stokes / Lonely Planet

© JAndriy Blokhin / Shutterstock

AS VISITORS TO JAPAN QUICKLY DISCOVER, THE PEOPLE HERE ARE ABSOLUTELY OBSESSED WITH FOOD.

kelp and *buta-niku* pork, live longest of all. That's not to say that Japanese cuisine doesn't have its fair share of deep-fried dishes, fatty comfort food and trashy fast food. Cravings for a cheeseburger, sugary sponge cake or fried chicken don't go unsatisfied here.

Tomes have been written about Japanese food, not least on the delights of sushi and the health-inducing properties of everything from shitake mushrooms to miso soup. This book covers these topics, but hopefully it goes beyond that, to reveal the areas of Japanese cuisine that go unheralded – its playfulness, its diversity, its quirky historical origins, its fascinating regional differences and specialisations, and above all its role in defining and revealing Japanese culture. Plus, you'll find pointers on etiquette and explanations to demystify food rituals. 'Let's eat,' as the Japanese say – '*Ittadekemasho!*'.

HISTORY of JAPANESE CUISINE

Today there are over 50 thousand million (yes, that's right) cups of instant noodles consumed annually in Japan.

Twenty-four-hour convenience stores vend tasteless plastic fare to students working so hard in cram schools that they don't care what they eat, and Western cuisine is creeping into many towns and cities with American-style burgers and high-end, creative international gastronomic restaurants. Yet, on the flip side of that, Japan's fascination with local food, traditional cuisine and home cooking remains as strong as ever. Nearly 10,000 years after the Japanese ate their first Venus clam, they can't stop living, breathing, talking and eating *washoku*.

EARLY BEGINNINGS

One can't help but feel the Japanese were predestined to be gourmands. Back in the early Jomon period, sometime between 7500BC and 5000BC, the first residents on the islands that were later to be called Japan, were living it up on shellfish sashimi. Not a bad diet for a group that had yet to discover the wheel. The remnants of their early feasts of hamaguri Venus clams have been discovered at the Natsushima shell mound in Yokosuka, in current-day Kanagawa prefecture. By 2000BC, they were hunting large fish, using the Japanese technical masterpiece, the toggle harpoon. Uni (sea anemone) became all the rage. Already, some 4000 years before the invention of the instant noodle, the basics of Japanese cuisine were beginning to take shape.

Towards the end of the Jomon period, the industrious folks of the island of Kyushu began to adopt a way of life markedly different from that of the northern islanders. They began wet rice farming. The next

sea change in Japanese cuisine came with contacts with China. Soon *komugi* (wheat) and *omugi* (barley) were added to the list of cultural and culinary imports. They provided essential winter sustenance, and were a backup in case the rice harvest failed. Also via China, some 300 years before they got Buddhism, the Japanese got primitive versions of udon wheat noodles and *shōyu* (soy sauce).

EARLY TRADING & ISOLATION

Chinese business people had been trading for centuries, and even the Portuguese had travelled with their *kasutera* sponge cake, during the Sengoku period 'Warring States'(1467–1568), but from the late 1600s Japan was closed. Limited trade was allowed through Nagasaki, when it was believed the Portuguese brought tempura and techniques for frying game, yet even they were booted out, in 1639.

© Universal History Archive / Getty Images

THE JAPANESE MEAL

The first written record of a formal Japanese meal was found during the Nara period (710–794AD) when Japan took on China's political structure with the Ritsuryō system between the late 7th and 10th centuries. This was the daikyo, the 'big feast'. It contained koi (carp), tai (sea bream), masu (trout), tako (octopus) and kiji (pheasant), seasoned with shoyu (soy sauce), sake, vinegar and salt. It was a luxury reserved exclusively for the ruling classes, and although it was simple technically, it gave rise to the complex ritual serving that came to characterise Japanese formal dining.

Above: Serving sake in 1860s Japan

Only the bachelors of the Dutch East India company were allowed to do business, setting up a brewery in the port enclave of Dejima off Nagasaki that was to be the sole opening to the West from 1641 to 1854.

TOKYO'S CULINARY RISE

By the end of the 18th century, citizens flocked to the country's new capital Edo (current-day Tokyo), which by then boasted a population of nearly a million. A massive food industry sprang up to feed the newcomers, and their august patrons, the residents of Edo-jo castle, with tempura and sushi leading the wave of culinary fashion. This is when the city's characteristic strong, salty broth developed, and soba buckwheat noodles soared in popularity. Many of modern-day Tokyo's finest restaurants, and indeed the metropolis' insatiable appetite for eating out, date back to the Edo era.

WESTERN INFLUENCE

When Commodore Matthew Perry led four gunboats of the US East India Squadron into Edo Bay in 1853, Japan's isolation was finally over.

Western fashions became all the rage, as did eating habits. Knives and forks appeared for the first time. The centuries-old Buddhist prohibition against eating beef was summarily ditched in favour of a 'modern' carnivorous diet, as Japanese gentlemen in Sebiro suits (from a Japanese pronunciation of 'Saville Row') tucked into beef with relish. Even the Emperor succumbed to the fad, stating in 1873, 'His Imperial Highness graciously considers the taboo [against meat eating] to be an

Left: A formal tea ceremony can last several hours

© Jose Fuste Raga / Getty Images

unreasonable tradition'. Favourite was the ubiquitous sukiyaki, which may have been introduced by Portuguese traders back in the Edo period.

With the advent of the 20th century came militarism, grinding poverty, World War, Hiroshima and Nagasaki, and the non-punitive post-war reconstruction by the Americans. Japan leapt back onto the world economic stage, big time. The Americans left Hersheys, Meriken-ko 'American wheat flour', *kohi* (coffee), and a renewed penchant for things Western that included *yoshoku* (Western-style) restaurants. These still survive today, many little changed in the last half century.

THE LOCAL FOOD INDUSTRY

The mixture of hard graft and invention that propelled Japan from devastation to world economic power status in just several decades, applied too to its domestic food industry. It was the age of the giants, Kirin, Suntory and Asahi, but its undisputed champion was Nisshin Seifun, the company that in 1958 introduced Chikin Ramen, and gave the world instant noodles. Chikin Ramen's success, and that of its competitors, was breathtaking. In the first year of sale, instant ramen sold 13 million units. A decade later it was shifting 13 million packs a year.

© SKPG_Payless / Shutterstock

Above: A factory worker holds up a box of Chikin Ramen in the 1960s **Opposite:** *Onsen-tamago*, eggs boiled in hot spring

THE FUTURE OF JAPANESE CUISINE

Where Japanese cuisine goes from here, only time will tell. An increase in gentrification, young, creative Japanese chefs putting inventive spins on traditional cuisine, evolving agricultural practices and an increasing influx of tourists from all over the globe all contribute to an ever-evolving food landscape. But it seems Japan will always be bound by a deep-rooted sense of food history, culture and tradition.

THE GREAT TEMPURA MYSTERY

Japan's best-known foreign import is tempura. Yet rarely has the origin of a Japanese word been mired in so much controversy. The 'standard' encyclopaedia definition is that it entered the language from Portuguese, some time in the late 16th century. Even here, however, food historians can't agree. Some say it refers to the Catholic Holy days – in Latin, the 'Quattuor Tempora' – when, four times a year, the Portuguese traders were forbidden from eating red meat. Thus, they ate battered shrimp. Some say it referred to the 'tempora' (time) each week that eating red meat was prohibited (i.e Friday). Another belief is that it's simply a corruption of the Portuguese word 'tempero' for 'cooking'.

Some Japanese historians – perhaps those with a nationalist, revisionist bent? – say it has nothing to do with the Portuguese, but originated, as a deep-fried rice snack, in China during the 8th to 9th century Tang dynasty. A third school suggests that tempura was first created in 9th century India, then called Tenjiku in Japanese. So it goes that Edo period satirical novelist, Santo Kyoden, on one of the rare occasions he wasn't locked up in chains for lampooning the Shogunate, gave the nickname Tempura to Tenjiku-ronin, a hapless masterless samurai, and it somehow got transferred to the food.

The least known theory comes also courtesy of Santo Kyoden. It is rumoured that, in a creative moment, he described the dish as 'tenjiku kara furatto kita' the thing which 'floated over and popped in from ancient India'. As this was a bit of a verbal mouthful, it got abbreviated to Ten-fu-ra. Thus, tempura was born, from poetry.

16

©Sankei Archive / Getty Images

©Susan Wright / Lonely Planet

THE LAND

The Japanese may cling desperately to the edges of a mountain-packed, densely populated archipelago with a paucity of arable soil (at least relative to size), but it doesn't seem to have hindered the development of its cuisine. Indeed, Japanese chefs have thrived in adversity, aided and abetted by some crafty agricultural techniques borrowed from the country's Korean and Chinese neighbours. The fish-filled oceans and rivers (at least historically so) provide the natural source of *washoku* staples, and the warm, north-flowing Kuroshio ocean current from the south brings a regular influx of exotic species, and the yearly migration of the valuable, exquisite Oceanic bonito. Rice is perfectly suited to the heavy rainfall of the *tsuyu* (rainy season), and even the thin alpine soils are at the perfect altitude (and therefore day-night temperature difference) for cultivation of buckwheat. Hokkaido's wide-open pastureland provides dairy produce and vegetables.

The only fly in the geo-culinary ointment is the tendency for volcanoes to suddenly erupt, and cataclysmic earthquakes to cruelly level farmland and city alike. However, the Japanese are far too serious about their food to let a little seismic chaos spoil their dinner. They even harness it to cook *onsen-ryōri*, hot-spa cuisine. *Onsen-tamago* – eggs poached in thermal waters, especially alkaline ones – are simply exquisite.

ZEN & the ART of GREEN TEA

The Buddhist traveller monk Eisei, who later founded the Rinzai sect of Zen Buddhism, brought green tea and Zen from China at the beginning of the Kamakura period (1185–1333AD). Although *shōjin-ryōri* (vegetarian food) had existed in some form since the 6th century, with the popularisation of Zen (which strongly demanded a spiritual practise even at the meal table), it became widespread.

Zen monks have long recognised the importance of food and the act of eating as part of their religious practice. Cooking and eating is considered a meditation and an opportunity for learning. When the great Zen master Dogen-zenji wrote his *Tenzo Kyokun, Instructions for the Zen Cook*, in 1237, as one might guess, his observations went beyond 'Take two eggs...'.

On the simple act of washing and cooking rice, he wrote, 'Keep your eyes open. Do not allow even one grain of rice to be lost. Wash the rice thoroughly, put it in the pot, light the fire and cook it'. There is an old saying that goes, 'See the pot as your own head; see the water as your life-blood'. On whipping up a quick lunch, he wrote, 'Maintain an attitude that tries to build great temples from ordinary greens...Handle even a single leaf of a green in such a way that it manifests the body of the Buddha'. Remember that when you next fix a pot of instant noodles.

THE TEA CEREMONY

Chanoyu ('water for tea') is usually translated as 'tea ceremony', but it's more like performance art, with each element – from the gestures of the host, the design of space and selection of utensils to the feel of the tea bowl in your hand, and, of course, the quality of the tea – all carefully designed to articulate an aesthetic experience. A formal tea ceremony might last hours and include several courses of food and drink, like a dinner party. The actual preparation and drinking of the tea follows a highly ritualised sequence: the utensils are carefully washed and presented; the tea bowl is held just so. It's an insistence on correctness that infuses much of the arts in Japan. Matcha, powdered green tea, features in the traditional tea ceremony and has a high caffeine kick.

'BEFORE YOU STUDY ZEN, A BOWL IS A BOWL AND TEA IS TEA. WHILE YOU ARE STUDYING ZEN, A BOWL IS NO LONGER A BOWL AND TEA IS NO LONGER TEA. AFTER YOU'VE STUDIED ZEN, A BOWL IS AGAIN A BOWL AND TEA IS TEA.'

ZEN 'KOAN' OR RIDDLE

SEASONING

© d3sign / Getty Images

Whereas Western cuisines with their markedly strong seasonings and distinctive sauces, often appeal initially to the olfactory sense, Japanese cuisine is unashamedly visual. This applies to every meal, from humble *shokudō* canteens, to high-class *kaiseki ryōtei*. If something looks like it has been plonked on a plate, you can guarantee it will taste poor. *Yosou* is the verb to 'dress up' or 'ornament' and is the formal word used to describe how food is arranged. Creating a harmony of colour, shape and texture is essential, and careful consideration is given to every element: the food itself, to the colour of the garnish and the shape of the bowl it is served in. And, of course, in best Zen tradition, there must be space or *ma*, that small element left forever to the imagination. Thus *kaiseki* dishes are never completely filled.

The Chinese-derived definition of a 'perfect meal', dating back to around the 3rd century BC, demands it contains the five colours – black (or purple), white, red (or orange), yellow and green. It should also use the five techniques (boiling, grilling, deep frying, steaming and serving raw) and contain the five essential tastes (sweet, salty, sour, bitter and peppery hot). The Japanese, in their famed manner of 'adopting and adapting',

SALT & VINEGAR PERFECTION

Since the Heian period (794–1185) salt, vinegar, sake and shōyu (soy sauce) have been the core seasonings at the heart of Japanese cuisine. Shio (salt) and su (vinegar) took pride of place, as practically both could be used for pickling, and vinegar removed the 'fishy' smell from seafood. In Japan's medieval past, umezu, sour-plum vinegar, was most commonly used, although before that yuzu, kabosu and sudachi citrons were used as vinegars.

The Kanji characters for 'shio' and 'ume' (of 'Umezu') when combined give the Japanese epicurean's favourite word ambai. 'Ambai ga ii' (literally 'the ambai is good') praises the perfect balance of seasonings, and, by extension, 'a perfect dish'. It is the highest praise.

© d3sign / Getty Images

Left: Adding soy sauce to a meal of rice and seafood

In 1908, Japanese chemist, Kikunae Ikeda, from the Tokyo Imperial University, uncovered the chemical basis of the taste 'umami' after he had been studying the Japanese broth, dashi, and trying to isolate the molecules behind its flavour. Umami, which can be loosely translated as 'delicious', is now recognised as one of the five basic tastes along with sweet, bitter, salty and sour.

embraced the concept, but replaced peppery hot (its echo still found only in *shichimi-togarashi* and *sansho*) with its own taste, umami.

Scientists have declared that umami is indeed a separate basic 'taste' with its own territory mapped out on taste buds dedicated to responding to glutamates, creating the *umami seibun* 'tastiness factor'. It refers to the 'tastiness' of the amino acids of MSG (found not only in *shokudō* kitchens, but naturally in *konbu* kelp and fresh tomatoes), and other amino acids and nucleotides in the *dashi* stock basics, *niboshi* and *katsuobushi*, and the sodium guanylate of dried shitake mushrooms.

Not surprisingly, the Japanese are proud of this complex, deeply rarefied cuisine, and the giving of gifts of food is very common. These vary from *omiyage* (souvenirs of trips in-country or overseas) to the mid-summer and year-end gift packages that companies present to cherished customers. Accompanying the gift-giving is Japan's now legendary (infamous?) obsession with packaging. Traditional Japanese wrapping may elevate even a small corner store purchase into a beautiful aesthetic package.

HOW the JAPANESE EAT

Japanese meals neither look nor taste like Western ones. They usually consist of a variety of separate, small dishes. These are all served at once, on a single lacquerware tray or table, with only miso soup and rice coming later. And there's always rice.The absence of, say, dramatic French-style sauces or intoxicating Indian spices means that, at first glance, Japanese cuisine can appear rather bland. This is in fact a reflection of how the Japanese perceive food, and by extension, seasoning. The Japanese classify most *seiyo-ryōri* or *yoshoku* Western dishes as *tashizan-ryōri* or cuisine created by addition of seasonings, and blendings of taste. By contrast, most *Nihon-ryōri* or *washoku* Japanese dishes fall into the category of *hikizan-ryōri*, where the natural seasonings in whatever ingredient is used must be artfully 'drawn out' by the chef. Only at the last minute, an addition of perhaps aromatic yuzu cit-ron, or *sanshō* prickly-ash pepper may be added, but this will always complement and enhance the natural flavours. It may take a while to adjust to this subtle delicacy, but once you do, you'll become a convert.

Left: Tempura, seaweed and soba noodles at a family gathering

BREAKFAST

The Japanese food day starts with *asa-go-han* ('the morning rice'). In the big cities this has become quite Westernised and you may find yoghurt and cereal or a slice of thick, bleached, sugary bread for toast. The traditional Japanese breakfast, however, is savoury, featuring lustrous rice, fried fish and that wonderfully aromatic miso soup.

The minute you visit a rural community, expect a step back in culinary time, as chairs and kitchen counters once more give way to zabuton cushions, tatami mats and low tables, and a more leisurely pace prevails. Eating a slow, simple breakfast of locally produced ingredients in a rural traditional *minka* (farmhouse) is a great luxury, and one that is slowly disappearing. If you get the chance, take it. The traditional breakfast always followed a farmer's calendar, early, early. And another great joy of dining with a family in the countryside is that there's the strong possibility that the young hosts will take off to tend the rice paddies, whilst the *Ojii-chan* (granddad) and *Obaa-chan* (grandma) fuss around and spoil you outrageously. More often than not they'll bring out futon, or lay out more zabuton, and everyone will take a much-needed post-prandial nap. In urban areas, breakfasts are the same indigestion-inducing high-speed affairs as in the West.

LUNCH

For *hiru-gohan* (lunch), ramen, soba and udon shops, company or school *shokudō* (canteens), or even the humble *konbini* (convenience stores) are all popular options. Eating lunch at home is very rare. In the cities, it's usually the women who will prepare not only breakfast, but also the bentō lunchboxes that they, their spouses and their children take to office and school. Schoolkids dread the totally uncool *hinomaru-bentō*: plain rice with a single umeboshi (pickled plum) at the centre, named after the Japanese flag.

DINNER

Ban-gohan (the evening meal) is the one the family is most likely to eat together, though this too often crumbles under the work and study pressures of modern urban life. If families dine out together, it will mostly be at a *fami-resu*, the 'family restaurant' chains serving inexpensive, at times inedible papier-mâché fare. They are rarely good, at best fair, but always affordable and handy. Couples without children and young adults are most likely to head off to an izakaya.

HOW TO USE CHOPSTICKS

Chopsticks, known as *ohashi*, are ubiquitous in Japan and are used to eat most dishes. If you struggle with getting the hang of them, here are a few pointers. There are a few social rules guiding proper usage of chopsticks in Japan, see page 43.

1

Hold your dominant hand with your thumb spread out from the rest of your palm, like your going to shake hands with someone.

2

Rest one chopstick on your palm in the space between your thumb and forefinger and close your thumb up to your palm.

3

Bend your ring and pinky fingers down and rest the chopstick on them.

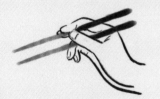

4

Hold the second chopstick in between your thumb and forefinger resting on your index finger, like you would do holding a pen.

5

Slide your middle finger down under the upper chopstick so it supports it.

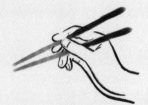

6

Move the upper chopstick up and down to grip food and pick it up.

Right: Women preparing food in an 18th century kitchen, by Kitagawa Utamaro

HOME COOKING

The *daidokoro* (kitchen), birthplace of so much marvellous Japanese cuisine, was the central focus of the daily life of a rural farmhouse. In the country, these would be large spaces (*daidokoro* means 'the big space'), with packed earth floors. In the cities, they were much smaller, a situation which remains the same today.

In Kyoto, the merchant's *machiya* townhouses were built long and thin to avoid taxation, which was calculated by the size of a property's frontage, earning them the nickname *unagi-no-nedokoro* ('places of the sleeping eels'). Even today, many traditional Kyoto kitchens are wholly impractical long, thin slivers, with cupboards set so high they have to be accessed via short, portable stepladders.

Traditional kitchens shared the same simple domestic set-up. There would always be a *kamado* (the wood or charcoal-burning stove that was used to heat the rice and boil water), with a small separate fire (the precursor of the heat-control switch) that allowed the different parts of the stove to be heated to different temperatures. Above the stove would be the kitchen's most important element, a strip of calligraphy obtained from the local Shinto shrine called the *hinoyoji-no-ofuda*, a protective amulet to ward off fires. Even today, these are very much in evidence, although the times of every single house being made of wood are long gone.

There would be no table, as kitchens were designed solely for preparation, and eating would be in a neighbouring tatami mat room. There would be basic utensils: the *suri-kogi* (mortar and pestle for grinding sesame), *o-tama* (ladles), *zaru* (sieves of either wood or metal), some simple Hocho knives, and metal *nabe* pans.

There would also possibly be a *mizuya-dansu*, the glass-fronted chest-of-drawers used for storing the multitude of specially shaped dishes that Japanese cooking demands, and also a wooden rectangular, sand-filled hibachi (hearth). The latter was used for heating, as an ever-ready source of fire. Suspended above the hibachi you would often find a *jizai-kagi* (wooden rig-and-pulley contraption), often in the shape of a fish, used for holding the cast iron *nabe* used in *nabemono*.

Naturally, one would find chopsticks – such an indelicate phrase for such elegant utensils. Traditionally, men's chopsticks were longer than women's (to fit their larger hands) and the low *ozen* (tables on which food was served), were slightly higher for women, so that the appropriate decorum could be maintained and the kimono-clad women didn't have to eat Quasimodo-fashion. Even today, a traditional wedding gift is a lacquerware chopstick set. Finally, the traditional kitchen would possess its symbolic utensil, the *shamoji*, the flat, oval-ended wooden spoon used for serving rice.

THE MODERN-DAY KITCHEN

In the '60s, when Japan discovered such modern artefacts as single-tub washing machines, hairdryers and the electric guitar (it was for a short while dubbed the *denki-shamoji*, the 'electric rice-spatula'), one might have expected there to be an avalanche of technical developments in the kitchen. Yet even today, some half a century later, the modern Japanese kitchen looks like a rather under-equipped, old-fashioned affair. OK, an electric *suihanki* (rice cooker) has been installed, with a *reizoko* (fridge), *keiko-to* (neon lighting bright enough to melt ones eyeballs), and perhaps a *denshi-renji* (microwave). Yet, in many cases, there's probably no dishwasher, no hotplate and cooking is most likely done on a two-ring gas stove that in the West has been long consigned to construction worker cabins and holiday caravans. The reason may well rest in the pervasive *danjo-shakai*, the male-dominated society. The country that brought you such technological marvels as the Honda two-stroke engine, the Walkman and the voice-activated robotic dog, did so courtesy of male designers looking towards male customers. The kitchen has still been, for the most part, sorely overlooked. It may be a telling sign that the kitchens of exclusive *ryotei* restaurants, which are largely run and staffed by males, are where you'll find design innovations in kitchen utensils that date back centuries.

HOSTING VS DINING OUT

To the Japanese, entertaining guests at home is anathema. If they do discuss throwing a homupaati (dinner party), it is inevitably in the tones of someone explaining an impending bout of highly embarrassing, potentially life-threatening surgery. The reason for this a combination of the esoteric – the cultural imperative that requires the separation of daily life (ke-no-hi) and the celebratory (hare-no-hi), and the practical – most Japanese people believe they live in usagi-goya ('rabbit huts') too small, cramped and full of family to show outsiders. This, combined with the endless opportunity for gai-shoku (eating out), makes it about as easy to get into a domestic kitchen as it is to get into the inner sanctum of the Imperial Palace.

A bowl of *nanakusa-gayu* (seven-herb rice soup)

COOKING METHODS

If Japanese kitchens haven't radically changed across the centuries, it comes as no surprise, then, that neither has the way in which food is prepared and served. Many families eat in the *obanzai* style, wherein the meal consists of several communal dishes from which diners pick and choose. These will be accompanied by *gohanmono* (rice dishes), and *shirumono* (miso) or *sunomono* clear soup. Really traditional households will still lay on a full restaurant-style spread, but as for a family of eight (not uncommon with both sets of grandparents in residence) this necessitates

preparing, then washing up countless dishes, it is fast losing favour. This labour-intensive system stems from the way in which each meal is required to contain most, if not all, the different representative forms of cooking: *nimono* (stewed, simmered) dishes, *yakimono* (broiled, grilled or pan-fried) dishes, *agemono* (deep-fried) and *mushimono* (steamed) dishes, *sunomono* (vinegared) and *aemono* (cooked salad) dishes, and, of course, *gohanmono* rice dishes. No wonder, then, that the one exception to this style of eating, the *nabemono* (one-pot dish) is so popular.

Above: A communal meal, with rice, miso, chicken and tea

JAPANESE KNIVES

Japanese kitchen knives are renowned for their quality, artisanship and beauty. Known as Wa-Bocho, traditional Japanese knives are typically made from high carbon steel, with the same hand-forging techniques once used to produce samurai swords. These premium-grade kitchen knives differ from Western knives in that they feature a bevelled blade – kabata – meaning the outer side of the blade is a bevelled edge while the inner side remains flat. This style enables extremely sharp and precise cutting and clean separation of food from the blade. Some of the main knives in Japanese cooking are:

GYUTOU (CHEFS' KNIFE)

The *gyutou* (cow sword) is an all-purpose blade, great for a variety of vegetables and meat.

SANTOKU (ALL-PURPOSE KNIFE):

A lighter, thinner choice, *santoku* means 'three virtues', which indicates that it can be used for meat, fish and vegetables.

PETTY (SMALL UTILITY KNIFE)

Petty knives are a smaller version of a *santoku* and are great for fine cutting tasks, such as for small vegetables and fruit.

NAKIRI (VEGETABLE KNIFE)

This square-shaped double-bevel blade is perfect for cutting all manner of vegetables.

YANAGI (SASHIMI KNIFE)

A long, thin, elegant fillet knife used by sushi masters for precision slicing of fish for sashimi and sushi.

今日の飯
ぷ
ひ
ら
め
こ
き
ん
ぱ
ち
か
ん
ぱ
ち

たこ

まごち

Left: Japanese chefs
hone their knife skills

When knife shopping in
Japan, head to Aritsugu
located in Kyoto's Nishiki
Market. Founded in
1560, Aritsugu was
originally involved in the
production of swords
and the blacksmith
skills have been passed
down over the years
through generation after
generation. It is known
as one of the best places
for kitchen knives in
Japan and has gained
the highest reputation
by top Japanese chefs.

31

Left: Tokyo's Omoide Yokocho ('Memory Lane') is packed with restaurants

WARIBASHI

The 'chopsticks that split' are ubiquitous in modern Japanese life. Enough are used, and discarded, each year to build roughly 30,000 homes, most of the raw materials coming from Japan's South-East Asian neighbours. If you don't wish to add to the environmental plunder, carry your own re-usable chopsticks (easily bought in Japan), and gently but firmly refuse the disposable variety with a polite but firm, 'waribashi wa kekko desu' ('thanks but no thanks'). If it causes a minor break in service, worry not – you haven't mortally offended anyone.

MADE FROM HAMMERED STAINLESS STEEL AND WITH A WOODEN HANDLE, THE **YUKIHIRA NABE** IS A JAPANESE COOKING POT **MUCH LOVED** BY PROFESSIONAL CHEFS

33

SEASONALITY

Take the *shun* (seasonality) out of Japanese cuisine, and it loses its soul. Japan is a country of natural beauty distinctly changing and food is a significant part of seasonal celebrations. The Japanese are keenly aware of seasonality and it is an integral part of not only food preparation and ingredients, but its presentation also.

Using the freshest local ingredients has long been a given in Japanese cuisine, from home-cooking to the poshest *ryōtei*, but chefs, in particular, will concentrate on the clear soup *suimono* and its topping, the *suikuchi* (often green shallots). When the customer opens the bowl of the *suimono*, they should be able to recognise the season. This is not always as easy as it sounds, as the only ingredient used in the clear soup garnish, or *koto* as it is called, was historically *yuzu* citron. The chef would choose it according to season, when its colour might be yellow or *aoyuzu* (green), or use the *yuzu no hana* flower, or even cut it to mimic the shape of seasonal imagery.

Today, *kinome* leaves from the *sanshō* prickly-ash and *fuki* buds, are commonly used, but it was the humble citron that gave the chefs their awareness of, and love for, seasonality.

Left: Japan's cherry blossom is world-famous

SPRING
(MARCH–MAY)

The new growth of spring finds its way onto tables in the form of *takenoko* (bamboo shoots) and *sansei* (mountain vegetables). Especially good if you're in the mountains.

SUMMER
(JUNE–AUGUST)

The Japanese summer is long, hot and very humid. Dishes consumed to beat the heat include *reimen* (cold ramen), *hiyashi-somen* (cold thin wheat noodles served in an ice bowl), *zaru soba* (cold soba noodles served on a bamboo tray with a dipping broth) and huge bowls of *kakigōri*, a shaved ice dessert topped with condensed milk, fruit-flavoured syrups or sweet *azuki* beans.

AUTUMN
(SEPTEMBER– NOVEMBER)

The first sign of autumn is silvery *sanma* (Pacific saury) on menus. Other delicacies include *matsutake* (mushrooms), ginkgo nuts, candied chestnuts and *shinmai*, the first rice of the harvest season.

WINTER
(DECEMBER– FEBRUARY)

Friends come together for steaming *nabe* (hotpot) dishes; this is also the season for fugu (pufferfish) and oysters. And perfect for *yumizake* – drinking sake while viewing the snow.

Above: Sake is used to toast special occasions, including weddings

CELEBRATING WITH FOOD

Sea bream pops up at each celebratory event in *honzen-ryori* (celebration cuisine), and every rite-of-passage, most notably in the marriage ceremony. Most contemporary Japanese weddings take place in huge wedding halls, with specially constructed sugar-candy Disneyesque 'chapels', Western-style buffet meals, several changes of clothes by the bride (wedding dress, kimono and evening gown are de rigeur), and a general lack of frivolity. To some degree, weddings are symbolic unions of families and a chance to cement business and social connections. Yet, even within a pseudo-Christian 'chapel', surrounded by guests clad in Western garb, the wedding couple will seal the marriage by exchanging sake cups and drinking sake in *sansankudo no sakazuki*, a Shinto ceremony dating back centuries before the birth of Christ.

A month after the arrival of a first child, he or she will be whisked off in swaddling clothes to a Shinto shrine for *omiya-mairi,* the first shrine visit, which once again will be marked by a sake toast. Thus, begins the life attached to food and drink. The majority of Japanese are born and marry Shinto, yet they die Buddhist. On the night preceding the funeral at the *otsuya* (wake), relatives and mourners are served *Butsu-ji*, Buddhist funerary cuisine. *Konnyaku* (konjac), *yuba* (the skin that forms when making tofu), tofu and vegetables are the main ingredients, with meat and fish strictly forbidden. At Japanese funerals, the custom is also to leave out a bowl of rice with chopsticks stuck upright, hence the strict taboo against leaving one's chopsticks in rice during everyday meals.

A FOOD CALENDAR

JANUARY

SHŌGATSU (NEW YEAR)

The celebratory year begins in homes and restaurants, with the multicourse, lavish, colourful *osechi-ryōri*. Families come together to eat and drink to health and happiness. The holiday is officially 1 to 3 January, but many businesses and attractions close the whole first week, and transport is busy. *Hatsu-mōde* is the ritual first shrine visit of the new year.

The other great New Year delicacy is *ozoni*, *mochi* served in soup. Its precise ingredients vary extensively from region to region. In Kansai, it is called *enman*, literally 'oval-full', but carrying the meaning of 'peace and harmony', and thus oval-shaped *mochigome* (glutinous rice) is used. Inhabitants of Western Japan also usually include *buri* (yellowtail). Usually *ozoni* is a clear soup, though in Kyoto *shiro miso* (sweet, white miso) is used.

FEBRUARY

SETSUBAN (3 FEBRUARY)

The Setsubun *matsuri* (festival) at shrines throughout the country feature worshippers and tourists gleefully peppering costumed *oni* (demons) with hard soybeans, to the cry of '*Oni wa soto, Fuku wa Uchi*' ('Out with the Demons, In with Good Luck'). The ceremony traditionally marks the end of winter. Householders scatter beans throughout their homes for similar protection against evil, and then, for added good luck, consume the number of beans equivalent to their age.

MARCH/APRIL

HINA MATSURI (3 MARCH)

This girls' day celebration involves *sekihan* (red rice) made from a mixture of glutinous and non-glutinous rice mixed with either *azuki* beans or *sasage* (black-eyed peas), which give it both sweetness and its characteristic pink colour. In addition to

A FOOD CALENDAR

sekihan, diamond-shaped *hishi-mochi* rice-cakes, *hinazushi* (with its shades of pink, yellow and brown) and white *shiro-zake* (a drink made of sake and rice malt) is commonly served and is said to ward off evil; there are prayers for good health.

SAKURA SEASON

Late March or early April sees the much-anticipated coming of the sakura (cherry blossoms). *Hanami*, the 'flower-viewing' parties, accompany the brief, glorious reign of the pink blossoms, transforming every inch of open space into a riot of alcohol-drenched, raucous contemplation of the evanescence of life and beauty. Actually, most attendees are too intent on consuming great quantities of cold beer and sake to notice the flowers.

MAY

TANGO-NO-SEKKU (5 MAY)

The Boys' Festival is a family affair to celebrate the healthy growth of boys and is celebrated with *Ise-ebi* (Japanese spiny lobster) cleverly carved into the shape of a *yaroi*, the samurai's traditional armour, and served on a bed of vinegared rice that resembles a flowing river. At the base of the stream are small fried fish, symbolising carp swimming valiantly upstream. Around the plates are iris leaves, representing swords. *Kashiwa-mochi* (pounded glutinous rice with a sweet filling, wrapped in an aromatic oak leaf) is also a traditional dish.

JULY

GION MATSURI

The star summer festival is Kyoto's Gion Matsuri, nicknamed *Hamo-matsuri*, the Pike-conger Festival, for the large quantities of the beast consumed during that time. Anyone unfortunate to be trapped in ultra-humid Kyoto over the summer heads to the village of Kibune, a small mountain settlement to the north, for the curious practise of *nagashi-somen*. Customers sit on *yuka* (straw platforms) set over the flowing, cool, clear mountain stream. A restaurant employee, perched handily upstream, drops thin white *somen* noodles into the river, which the downstream guests deftly pluck from the cold waters with chopsticks, and dip into a chilled *tsuyu* (dipping sauce).

O-BON (13–15 JULY)

The Buddhist equivalent of All Souls' Day is celebrated in most areas (in some a month later) when

the spirits of the dead return to this realm. Obviously, they're a bit peckish after the trip from the netherworld, so families gather (as they do at New Year) to pay respects, commune with their deceased ancestors, dance outdoors beneath lanterns, and eat. There's no specific O-bon cuisine, but a deceased relative's favourite dishes may be placed, in miniature, before the family's Buddhist shrine and its Shinto kamidana ('god-shelf' or altar).

SEPTEMBER/ OCTOBER

TSUKIMI

Full moons in September and October call for *tsukimi* (moon-viewing gatherings). People eat *tsukimi dango* – *mochi* (pounded rice) dumplings, round like the moon, to celebrate the autumn harvest. In a fast-food joint, you may encounter a Tsukimi Burger at this time.

NOVEMBER

SHICHI-GO-SAN MATSURI (15 NOVEMBER)

This festival requires families with children aged seven, five or three to go to their local shrine. Boys of five are decked out in the male kimono or *hakama*, while girls of seven and three wear their best kimono; they are often appeased with in-season freshly roasted *kuri* (chestnuts), either served hot or as-is, from miniature trucks parked outside the shrine, or in *kuri-gohan* (chestnut rice) prepared at home.

DECEMBER

OLD YEAR'S NIGHT (31 DECEMBER)

The year finishes with the ringing 108 times of the gong, *Joya-no-kane*, to relegate the traditional 108 Buddhist sins into a past life. The population heads en masse for the country's Shinto shrines to offer prayers and alms to guide them into the New Year. Inevitably, it's a freezing midwinter night, and the warm *amazake* (sweet sake) helps keep out the winter chill.

The first dish of the New Year will be *toshikoshi* soba (long buckwheat noodles) symbolising long life and wealth, as soba dough was once used by gold traders to collect gold dust. To cries of *'Yoi o-toshi wo'* ('Have a happy New Year') and *'Akemashite Omedeto gozaimasu'* ('Happy New Year'), the eating and celebration continues anew…

Left: Eating out in Japan is a pleasure but there are rules to follow

© SJohnnyGreig / Getty Images

ETIQUETTE

Getting into a restaurant or party hall poses the first etiquette challenge. Who goes first? This will usually be the eldest person or the guest of honour. Most likely it will be you. Remember to bow as you're invited to go in first. The host will probably gesture with an open palm which direction you should follow. Bow slightly in thanks, but don't bow too deeply. Being overly polite is probably worse than not bowing enough. For a start, it slows everyone down in getting in for the grub, and it's also a subtle (and very Japanese) way of suggesting someone is an idiot.

Negotiating the *genkan* (entranceway) is the next hurdle. Taking your shoes off may require a little tightrope-walking balancing trick, but don't be tempted to put one stockinged foot on the floor while you struggle with a recalcitrant boot. It defeats the purpose of removing your shoes. Try to slip directly into the room slippers that are facing you. Once inside, walk to the tatami straw-matted room... and take your footwear off again. No slippers on the tatami, please.

The senior guest will be ushered to the low table, and invited to sit at the *kamiza* (the seat of honour) nearest the tokonoma

41

(alcove). It probably has the best view of the garden and the *kakejiku (*hanging scroll) or ikebana (flower-arrangement) in the tokonoma. Often at this stage there may be some debate amongst the guests over who the senior guest actually is, with hefty scientific calculations about age, status and seniority, accompanied with lots of please-you-sit-theres and oh-no-I-couldn't-possiblys.

Things usually kick off with the toast, perhaps accompanied by a short speech, but more often than not just a quick '*Kanpai*!'. Even if you don't drink, you're expected to pretend to take a sip. Someone will probably offer to fill your glass, in the drinking custom known as *henpai*. It may be the host, or perhaps someone younger than you, or, especially if you're a man, a nearby female. The done thing is to lift your glass from the table, tilt it towards the person offering you the beer, wait till the glass is filled, then put it down, and reciprocate. Then you drink together. This will continue through the meal, or party, often with several people coming to fill your glass. The polite way to signal you're in danger of keeling over is to cover your glass with

Above: Toasts usually kick off a formal meal in Japan

42

your hand. Before eating, you will be offered an *oshibori* (hot towel, or cooled in summer) to wipe your hands with. It's considered rather boorish to use it to wipe your brow, but many people do that anyway.

Then, of course, come the *ohashi* (chopsticks). A little practise before you start never hurts. While there is a rather complex etiquette about how you hold the chopsticks, it's not worth losing sleep over. Many young Japanese adopt the casual, easiest way, and non-Japanese guests will be forgiven for doing the same thing. There are a few no-nos, however. *Mayoibashi*, the 'lost and wandering' chopsticks, where you dab uncertainly at different dishes is frowned upon. Passing food from your chopsticks directly to someone else's is strictly taboo, as it mimics Japanese funerary practise. So does sticking chopsticks vertically into a bowl of white rice. Pointing at someone with chopsticks, despite the vehemence of your conviction, is not polite.

When you remove a food item to your plate from a communal bowl, it is polite to use the opposite, thick end of your chopsticks. This culinary backhand is easy to forget, not least when you're ravenous. Should you inadvertently catapult a piece of raw squid across the banquet table, worry not. The Japanese themselves have been known to do this. Simply say '*Shitsurei-shimashita*' ('Forgive me for having committed a rudeness').

ESSENTIAL ETIQUETTE PHRASES

Here are a few handy phrases to help negotiate dining:

- Before you eat, say '***Itadakimasu***', and after '***Gochisosama-deshita***'. The latter is a rather beautiful invocation, derived from Buddhist practice, which gives thanks to the cooks who ran around to gather ingredients, though many Japanese themselves are unaware of this. In informal situations it may be abbreviated to *Gochisosama*.
- A very common practice is saying '***Oishii***' ('That's delicious') after the first mouthful of any dish, regardless of its quality.

- The most serious threat to your corporeal and digestive wellbeing is likely to be the generosity of your Japanese hosts, who are given to plying guests with food and drink well beyond the realm of what is sane or sober. It is often difficult to refuse, but an oft repeated '***Mo ippai desu***' ('I'm full'), '***Tabesugimashita***' ('I ate too much') or '***Nomisugimashita***' ('I drank too much') should at least pause the deluge.

WHERE & HOW to EAT

It's not hard to get a great feed in Japan. You can eat well on any budget, whether you're looking to slurp back noodles in a cheap and cheerful ramen bar, snack on plates of sushi while propped up at the counter chatting to the chefs, or spend the evening appreciating the art of high-end *kaiseki* cuisine in a private dining room of a traditional building.

With the exception of *shokudō* and izakaya, most Japanese restaurants concentrate on a speciality cuisine. For example, you typically go to a *ramen-ya* (ramen restaurant) for ramen and a *sushi-ya* for sushi. The bigger cities around the country have a good spread of everything, including many international options; in the smaller and more rural towns, you'll mostly find local cuisine. Usually only the high-end restaurants require advance booking. For really popular dining spots in the big cities – including well-known tiny ramen and sushi bars or local institutions – you may need to queue at peak times.

PLACES TO EAT

IZAKAYA

Japanese-style pubs serving small plates to go with sake or beer; open 5pm to late.

SUSHI—YA

Counter-seating joints (both casual and fancy) specialising in sushi; open for lunch and dinner.

KISSATEN

Old-school coffee shops; come before 11am for 'morning sets' of discounted coffee, toast and a hard-boiled egg.

SHOKUDŌ

Inexpensive establishments that serve set meals of home-cooking classics; open for lunch and dinner. Meals usually include a main dish, rice and miso soup.

KONBINI

Ubiquitous 24-hour convenience stores stocked with sandwiches, bento (boxed meals, which you can ask to have microwaved) and onigiri (rice-ball snacks).

RYŌTEI

The highest class of Japanese restaurant, typically in a traditional building and set around a garden.

DEPARTMENT STORES

The upper levels have restaurants, often branches of famous ones; reliably good food and reasonably priced, usually with English menus. Takeaway and deli dishes can be purchased in the glorious food halls in the basement.

Left: A late-night
restaurant in Osaka

RESTAURANT ETIQUETTE

When you enter a restaurant in Japan, the staff will likely all greet you with a hearty '*Irasshai!*' (Welcome!) In all but the most casual places, where you seat yourself, the waitstaff will next ask you '*Nan-mei sama?*' (How many people?). Indicate the answer with your fingers, which is what the Japanese do. You may also be asked if you would like to sit at a *zashiki* (low table on the tatami), at a *tēburu* (table) or the *kauntā* (counter). Once seated you will be given an *oshibori* (hot towel), a cup of tea or water (this is free) and a menu.

In many high-end and sushi restaurants, there are generally two ways to order: *omakase* (chef's choice) and *okonomi* (your choice). It's common for high-end restaurants to offer nothing but *omakase* – the equivalent of a chef's tasting course – usually two or three options of different value. (Pricier doesn't necessarily mean more food; it often means more luxurious ingredients.)

Most other restaurants will hand you a menu and expect you to choose what you like. If there's no English menu (and you're game), you can ask for the server's recommendation '*O-susume wa nan desu ka?*' and give the okay to whatever he or she suggests.

When your food arrives, it's the custom to say '*Itadakimasu*' (literally 'I will receive' but closer to 'bon appétit' in meaning) before digging in. All but the most extreme type-A chefs will say they'd rather have foreign visitors enjoy their meal than agonise over getting the etiquette right. Still, there's nothing that makes a Japanese sushi chef grimace more than out-of-towners who over-season their food – a little soy sauce and wasabi go a long way.

Often a bill is placed discreetly on your table after your food has been delivered. If not, catch your server's eye with a '*sumimasen*' (excuse me) and ask for the check by saying, '*o-kaikei onegaishimasu*'. Payment, even at high-end places, is often settled at a counter near the entrance, rather than at the table. On your way out, it's polite to say '*Gochisō-sama deshita*' (literally 'It was a feast'; a respectful way of saying you enjoyed the meal) to the staff.

© Vincent St. Thomas / Shutterstock

NO ENGLISH MENU? NO PROBLEM

If you're generally an adventurous (or curious) eater, don't let the absence of an English menu put you off. Instead, tell the staff (or ideally the chef), 'omakase de onegaishimasu' ('I'll leave it up to you').

This works especially well when you're sitting at the counter of a smaller restaurant or izakaya, where a rapport naturally develops between the diners and the cooks. It's best said with enthusiasm and a disarming smile, to reassure everyone that you really are game. This isn't just a tip for tourists: Japanese diners do this all the time. Menus might not reflect seasonal dishes, and odds are the chef is working on something new that he or she is keen to test out on the willing.

EATING ETIQUETTE

If you only remember one thing, make it this: do not stick your chopsticks upright in a bowl of rice or pass food from one pair of chopsticks to another – both are reminiscent of Japanese funeral rites. But there are other lessons to learn.

When serving yourself from a shared dish, it's polite to use the back end of your chopsticks (i.e. not the end that goes into your mouth) to place the food on your own small dish.

Lunch is one of Japan's great bargains; however, restaurants can only offer cheap lunch deals because they anticipate high turnover. Spending too long sipping coffee after finishing your meal might earn you dagger eyes from the kitchen.

It's perfectly OK, even expected, to slurp your noodles. They should be eaten at whip speed, before they go soggy (letting them do so would be an affront to the chef); that's why you'll hear diners slurping, sucking in air to cool their mouths.

Eating and walking at the same time is considered impolite in Japan, as it goes against the etiquette of *'ikkai ichi dousa'* – which loosely translates as doing 'one thing at a time'. Finish your onigiri while standing out the front of the convenience store or find somewhere to sit down to eat your bento, otherwise you might elicit some stares of disapproval.

51

© Jonathan Stokes / Lonely Planet

© Rebecca Milner / Lonely Planet

ebi-katsu · 海老カツ
breaded and fried prawns

katsu-don · かつ丼
rice topped with a fried pork cutlet

katsu-karē · カツカレー
rice topped with a fried pork cutlet and curry

omu-raisu · オムライス
omelette wrapped around fried rice, topped with ketchup

oyako-don · 親子丼
rice topped with egg and chicken

ten-don · 天丼
rice topped with tempura prawns and vegetables

yaki-zakana teishoku · 焼き魚定食
grilled fish set meal

SHOKUDŌ

Shokudō (食堂) are casual, inexpensive establishments that serve comforting meals – similar to what might be called a diner in the US. These offer quick and easy meals, and usually enough variety to please everyone (including children). *Shokudō* are everywhere, and especially near train stations and tourist sights. They often have plastic food models displayed in their windows; in a pinch, if there's no English menu, beckon the wait staff and point to what you want.

One thing to order at a *shokudō* is a *teishoku* (定食), a set meal with one main dish (such as grilled fish) along with rice, miso soup and pickles. Other likely menu items include various *donburi* (どんぶり or 丼; large bowls of rice with meat or fish piled on top) and *katsu* (カツ) dishes, where the main is crumbed and deep fried.

IZAKAYA

Izakaya (居酒屋) translates as 'drinking house' — the Japanese equivalent of a pub — and you'll find them all over Japan.

Visiting an izakaya is a great way to dig into Japanese culture. Your evening will involve dinner and drinks all in one: food is ordered for the table a few dishes at a time, along with rounds of beer, sake or *shōchū* (a strong distilled alcohol often made from potatoes). While the vibe is lively and social, it's perfectly acceptable to go by yourself and sit at the counter. If you don't want alcohol, it's fine to order a soft drink instead (but it would be strange to not order at least one drink).

There are traditional, family-run izakaya, often with rustic interiors, that serve sashimi and grilled fish to go with sake. There there are large, cheap chains, popular with students, that often have a healthy (make that, unhealthy) dose of Western pub-style dishes (such as chips and pizza slices); there's usually a buzzer at the table to call wait staff and often a tablet for ordering food. You'll also find gastronomic and stylish izakaya with creative menus. A night out at an average izakaya should run ¥4000 to ¥8000 per person, depending on how much you drink. Chains often have deals where you can pay a set price for a certain amount of dishes and free drinks.

Note that izakaya often levy a small cover charge, called *otoshi*, of a few hundred yen per person. In exchange, you'll be served a small dish of food to snack on until the kitchen can prepare your order. But no, you can't pass it up even if you don't want to eat it!

FUGU

This Japanese pufferfish may be a delicacy, but its ancient nickname is teppo *('the pistol') from its tendency to bump off careless eaters. Its active ingredient is tetrodoxin: clear, tasteless, odourless poison 13 times stronger than arsenic. One* ma-fugu *contains enough to kill 33 people. Specially trained chefs remove (most of) the poison, leaving just enough to numb your lips. It goes without saying — you don't want to get on the wrong side of your fugu chef.*

KONBINI (CONVENIENCE STORE)

Convenience stores live up to their name in Japan like nowhere else. There are over 50,000 stores dotted across the country – you can't walk more than a block without spotting one or two (sometimes directly across the road from each other)– and most are open 24 hours a day, seven days a week. If you're in need of a quick meal or snack, they're a godsend. You can fuel up on sandwiches, baguettes stuffed with yakisoba (fried soba noodles), oni-giri (rice balls) with common fillings such as tuna and mayo or salmon, a range of bento (which staff can heat up for you), instant ramen noodle bowls (with hot-water thermoses to fill them up with), and plenty of crisps, chocolates, Pocky snacks, etc. They also sell a range of hot and cold drinks, including coffee, vitamin drinks and alcohol.

DEPAATO (DEPARTMENT STORE)

The idea of dining in a department store may not sound too appealing but Japanese department stores, especially those in large cities such as Tokyo or Kyoto, are loaded with good dining options.

On their basement floors, you'll find *depachika* (from the English word 'department' and the Japanese word *chika*, which means 'underground'). A good *depachika* is like an Aladdin's cave of gustatory delights. Even if you're not hungry, it's worth perusing these basement food halls to drool over the assort-ments of sushi, bento, delicate *wagashi* (Japanese sweets), tempting pastries and breads, and beautifully presented fruits and vegetables – some with eye-watering price tags.

Meanwhile, on their upper floors, you'll usually find a *resu-toran-gai* (restaurant city) that includes restaurants serving all the Japanese standards – sushi, noodles, *tonkatsu* (deep-fried breaded pork cutlet), tempura – along with a few international restaurants, usually French, Italian and Chinese.

YATAI (FOOD CARTS)

Yatai pop up in many towns around Japan, at festivals, and lining the path to shrines at week-ends. Traditional favourite street snacks include *tako-yaki* (grilled octopus dumplings), *taiyaki* (little cakes shaped like fish and filled with *azuki* bean paste, or other sweet fillings) and yakitori (grilled chicken on skewers). If you're really hungry, you might even try an *amerikan-doggu* – a hot dog on a stick.

IZAKAYA STAPLES

agedashi-tōfu · 揚げだし豆腐
deep-fried tofu in a dashi (fish) broth

edamame · 枝豆
salted and boiled fresh soy beans

gyōza · 餃子
pan-fried dumplings typically filled with
pork mince, cabbage and vegetables

hiyayakko · 冷奴
a cold block of tofu with soy sauce and
spring onions

jaga-batā · ジャガバター
baked potatoes with butter

kara-age · 唐揚げ
fried chicken

moro-kyū · もろきゅう
sliced cucumbers and chunky barley miso

niku-jaga · 肉ジャガ
beef and potato stew

sashimi mori-awase · 刺身盛り合わせ
a selection of sliced sashimi

shio-yaki-zakana · 塩焼魚
a whole fish grilled with salt

tamagoyaki · 玉子焼き
a fried and rolled omelette cut into pieces

yaki-onigiri · 焼きおにぎり
a triangle of grilled rice with yakitori sauce

WHAT TO EAT

YAKITORI

Putting away skewers of yakitori (charcoal-grilled chicken, but vegetables are served, too), along with beer, is a popular after-work ritual. Most *yakitori-ya* (*yakitori* restaurants) are convivial counter joints where the food is grilled over hot coals in front of you. It's typical to order a few skewers at a time. They're usually priced around ¥100 to ¥200 a piece; one order may mean two skewers (and thus may mean double the price). The chef will ask if you want your skewers seasoned with *shio* (salt) or *tare* (sauce). *Yakitori-ya* are often located near train stations and are best identified by a red lantern outside (and the smell of grilled chicken). Many can be found clustered under the arches of the swath of railway tracks and the raised expressway running from Yūrakuchō to Shimbashi in Tokyo. They are among some of Tokyo's most atmospheric places to grab a quick meal and frothy beer.

kawa · 皮
chicken skin

negima · ねぎま
pieces of white meat alternating with leek

piiman · ピーマン
small green capsicums (peppers)

rebā · レバー
chicken livers

sasami · ささみ
skinless chicken-breast pieces

shiitake · しいたけ
Japanese mushrooms

tama-negi · 玉ねぎ
round white onions

tebasaki · 手羽先
chicken wings

tsukune · つくね
chicken meatballs

yaki-onigiri · 焼きおにぎり
grilled rice ball

Left: A platter of
maki-zushi

SUSHI

Sushi (寿司 or 鮨) is raw fish and rice seasoned with vinegar. Today sushi is widely associated with fresh fish, but the dish originated as a way to make fish last longer – the vinegar in the rice was a preserving agent. Older styles of sushi were designed to last for days, and have that heavy tang of fermentation. These include *hako-zushi* or *oshi-zushi* ('box' or 'pressed' sushi), made by pressing fish onto a bed of heavily vinegared rice in a wooden mould with a weighted top; sushi in this style is still eaten frequently in western Japan.

Sushi evolved dramatically in 19th- and early 20th-century Tokyo. Tokyo Bay provided a steady stream of fresh seafood, making preservation less crucial; more importantly, sanitation improved. Sushi became a sort of fast food: deft-handed chefs quickly formed bite-sized blocks of rice and pressed slivers of fish atop for the new class of hungry urbanites. This style – now the most common style and what most people think of when they think of sushi – is called *nigiri-zushi*, which means hand-formed sushi.

Common *nigiri-zushi* toppings (called *neta*) include *ama-ebi* (sweet shrimp), *hamachi* (yellowtail), *ika* (squid), *katsuo* (bonito), *maguro* (tuna) and *toro* (fatty tuna belly meat). In truth not all *neta* are raw fish: you many encounter *anago* (conger eel) that has been grilled and lacquered in a sweet soy-sauce glaze; *tako* (octopus) that has been boiled; or *hotate* (scallops) that have been seared – among others. The same shops that specialise in *nigiri-zushi* will also serve *maki-zushi* (with the rice and *neta* rolled together in laver – edible seaweed). Delicacies such as *ikura* (salmon roe) and *uni* (sea-urchin roe) are served *asa gunkan-maki* ('battleship rolls'; it will make sense when you see it!).

Unless otherwise instructed by the chef (who may have pre-seasoned some pieces), you can dip each piece lightly in shōyu (soy sauce), which you pour from a small decanter into a low dish specially provided for the purpose. *Nigiri-sushi* is usually made with wasabi, so if you'd prefer it without, order *wasabi-nuki*. Sushi is one of the few foods in Japan that is perfectly acceptable to eat with your hands (even at high-end places!). Slices of *gari* (pickled ginger) are served to refresh the palate.

Right: Fresh *maki-zushi* and *nigiri-zushi*

YOU CAN EAT SUSHI WITH YOUR HANDS,
EVEN at HIGH—END PLACES

At an average *sushi-ya*, a meal should run between ¥2000 and ¥6000 per person. You can order à la carte – often by just pointing to the fish in the refrigerated glass case on the counter. But the most economical way to eat sushi is to order a set, usually of around 10 to 12 pieces, which may be served all at once or piece by piece. Sets usually come in three grades: *futsū* or *nami* (regular), *jō* (special) and *toku-jō* (extra-special). The price difference is determined more by the value of the ingredients than by volume. Sushi restaurants often also serve *chirashi-zushi* (bite-sized pieces of seafood scattered on a bowl of vinegar-seasoned rice); this too tends to be offered at different grades (using the same terms). Of course you can spend much much more at a high-end *sushi-ya*, where an *omakase* (chef's choice) course of seasonal delicacies could run over ¥25,000 per person. Sushi can also be had very cheaply, at *kaiten-zushi* (回転寿司), where ready-made plates of sushi (about ¥150 to ¥350 each) are sent around the restaurant on a conveyor belt. Here, there's no need to order, just grab whatever looks good (though you can usually order from the menu too, if you don't see what you want). The plates are generally colour-coded by price and the staff will tally up your used plates for the bill at the end of the meal.

SUKIYABASHI JIRO

Exclusive sushi restaurant Sukiyabashi Jiro in Tokyo's Ginza district is renowned as being one of the hardest restaurant reservations to get in the world. The tiny basement restaurant seats just 10 at its counter and is run by nonagenarian owner Jiro Ono, who starting making sushi when he left home at the age of nine. Sukiyabashi Jiro's reputation and popularity only grew when it hosted US President Obama in 2014, who sat alongside Japanese Prime Minister Shinzo Abe at the wooden counter. Jiro is widely regarded as one of the most skilled sushi chefs in the world and his restaurant had earned three Michelin stars every year since 2007. That is, until it was removed from the Michelin guide in 2020 as it was no longer accepting reservations from the general public due to overwhelming demand and limited spaces. For overseas visitors, you can try your luck getting a reservation if you go through a top hotel concierge very early in advance; be prepared to shell out plenty of yen for the experience. Otherwise, learn about the sushi mastery of Jiro Ono in the 2011 documentary Jiro Dreams of Sushi.

ama-ebi · 甘海老
sweet shrimp

anago · 穴子
conger eel

chū-toro · 中とろ
medium-grade fatty tuna

ebi · 海老
prawn or shrimp

hamachi · はまち
yellowtail

ika · いか
squid

ikura · イクラ
salmon roe

kai-bashira · 貝柱
scallop

kani · かに
crab

katsuo · かつお
bonito

maguro · まぐろ
tuna

tai · 鯛
sea bream

tamago-yaki · 玉子焼き
slightly sweetened rolled omelette

toro · とろ
the choice cut of fatty tuna belly

uni · うに
sea-urchin roe

DODGING PARASITES

One should be a little wary when eating sashimi (raw fish), as the very cheapest fish have been known to harbour the parasites anisakis: roundworms with a penchant for burrowing into your stomach wall to reproduce. Fortunately, instances of this are extremely rare. Common sense will tell you what's safe and what isn't. If raw fish smells too 'fishy', and you're in a less than salubrious establishment, play it safe. Good news is that su (vinegar) and wasabi (Japanese horseradish) are to fish parasites what Kryptonite is to Superman.

SUKiYAKi & SHABU—SHABU

Both sukiyaki (すき焼き) and shabu-shabu (しゃぶしゃぶ) are hotpot dishes, cooked by diners at the table; the same restaurant usually serves both (but may be known for one or the other). For sukiyaki, thin slices of beef are briefly simmered in a broth of *shōyu* (soy sauce), sugar and sake and then dipped in raw egg (you can skip the last part, though it makes the marbled beef taste even creamier).

For shabu-shabu, thin slices of pork and/or beef are swished around in boiling broth – shabu-shabu is the onomatopoeia for the sound of the meat being swished – then dipped in either a *goma-dare* (sesame sauce) or ponzu (citrus and soy sauce). In either case, a healthy mix of veggies and tofu are added to the pot a little bit at a time, followed by noodles at the end. So while sukiyaki and shabu-shabu can seem expensive (from around ¥3500 per person to upwards of ¥12,000 for premium beef), it is an all-inclusive meal.

One party shares the pot and the minimum order is usually two (though some places do lunch deals for solo diners). The waitstaff will set everything up for you and show you what to do.

62

TEMPURA

Tempura is seafood (fish, eel or prawns) and vegetables (such as pumpkin, green pepper, sweet potato or onion) lightly battered and deep-fried in sesame oil. Season by dipping each piece lightly in salt or a bowl of *ten-tsuyu* (broth for tempura) mixed with grated daikon (Japanese radish).

At a speciality restaurant, tempura is served as a set (all at once, with rice and soup) or as a course, with pieces delivered one at a time freshly cooked; you can order extras on top of the set or course, but rarely just à la carte. A tempura meal can cost between ¥1500 and ¥10,000, depending on the pedigree of the shop. *Shokudō* often serve cheaper *ten-don* (tempura on rice) dishes. Tempura can also often be ordered as a side dish at izakaya and noodle restaurants.

RAMEN

Ramen originated in China, but its popularity in Japan is legendary. If a town has only one restaurant, odds are it's a ramen shop.

Your basic ramen is a big bowl of crinkly egg noodles in broth, served with toppings such as char siu (sliced roast pork), *moyashi* (bean sprouts) and *menma* (fermented bamboo shoots). The broth can be made from pork or chicken bones or dried seafood; usually it's a top-secret combination of some or all of the above, falling somewhere on the spectrum between *kotteri* (thick and fatty – a signature of pork bone ramen) or *assari* (thin and light).

It's typically seasoned with *shio* (salt), *shōyu* (soy sauce) or hearty miso – though at less orthodox places, anything goes. Most shops will specialise in one or two broths and offer a variety of seasonings and toppings. Another popular style is *tsukemen*, noodles that come with a dipping sauce (like a really condensed broth) on the side.

Given the option, most diners get their noodles *katame* (literally 'hard', but more like al dente). If you're really hungry, ask for *kaedama* (another serving of noodles), usually only a couple of hundred yen more.

Well-executed ramen is a complex, layered dish – though it rarely costs more than ¥1000 a bowl. Costs are minimised by fast food–style service: often you order from a vending machine (you'll get a paper tick-

et, which you hand to the chef); water is self-serve. Many *ramen-ya* (ramen restaurants) also serve fried rice and *gyōza* (dumplings).

chāhan · 炒飯
fried rice

chāshū-men · チャーシュー麺
ramen topped with slices of roasted pork

gyōza · 餃子
dumplings, usually fried

miso ramen · みそラーメン
ramen with miso-flavoured broth

ramen · ラーメン
soup and egg noodles topped with meat and vegetables

tsuke-men · つけ麺
ramen noodles with soup on the side

SOBA & UDON

© Izumo Soba

Soba are thin brown buckwheat noodles (which may or may not be cut with wheat), while udon are thick white wheat noodles. Some restaurants may specialise in one or the other; other places will serve both. In general, eastern Japan tends to favour soba, while western Japan leans towards udon. There are also many regional variations.

Cheap noodle shops, where a meal costs less than ¥1000, are everywhere. At better shops, the noodles will be handmade from premium flours and mountain spring water (and will cost twice as much). But even at their most refined, noodles are a reasonably affordable meal.

Both soba and udon may be served in a hot broth that is flavoured with bonito, kelp, soy sauce and mirin (sweet sake). They may also be served cooled with dipping sauce (a more condensed broth) on the side, to which you can add such aromatics as spring onions or wasabi. The weather may be a deciding factor but so is personal preference: if a place is famous for its noodles, many customers would order them chilled, to better appreciate the flavour. (Also cooled noodles won't go mushy like those in hot broth, so can be savoured rather than scoffed).

ebi-ten soba/udon · 海老天そば/うどん
soba/udon noodles in hot broth topped
with prawn tempura

kake soba/udon · かけそば/うどん
soba/udon noodles in hot broth

kitsune soba/udon · きつねそば/うどん
soba/udon noodles with fried tofu

mori soba/udon · もりそば/うどん
cooled soba/udon served with a condensed dipping broth on the side

tempura soba/udon · 天ぷらそば/う
どん
soba/udon noodles with tempura
prawns

tsukimi soba/udon · 月見そば/うどん
soba/udon noodles with raw egg

te-uchi · 手打ち
handmade

to-wari soba · 十割そば
soba made with 100% buckwheat (not
cut with wheat)

When you order cooled noodles, the
restaurant will often bring you a small
kettle of hot water (the slightly starchy
water used to boil the noodles). Pour it
in the cup with the remaining dipping
sauce and enjoy it like a hot broth.

Left: Tonkatsu comes with an unusual and addictive sauce

TONKATSU

Tonkatsu is a pork cutlet coated in panko crumbs and deep-fried, almost always served as a set meal that includes rice, miso soup and a heaping mound of shredded cabbage. It is seasoned with tonkatsu sauce, a curious (and highly addictive) ketch-up-y condiment, or *karashi* (hot spicy yellow mustard). At around ¥1200 to ¥2500 a meal, it's perfect for when you want something hearty and filling. The best tonkatsu is said to be made from *kurobuta* (Black Berkshire pork) from Kagoshima.

When ordering at a speciality shop, you can choose between *rōsu* (a fattier cut of pork) and *hire* (a leaner cut). Tonkatsu and other crumbed and fried dishes are often served at *shokudō*.

hire katsu · ヒレかつ
tonkatsu fillet

katsu-don · かつ丼
rice topped with a fried pork cutlet

katsu-karē · カツカレー
rice topped with a fried pork cutlet and curry

tonkatsu teishoku · とんかつ定食
a set meal of tonkatsu, rice, *miso-shi-ru* (bean-paste soup) and shredded cabbage

rōsu katsu · ロースかつ
tonkatsu pork loin

© PRImageFactory / Getty Images

OKONOMIYAKI

Okonomiyaki is a dish that flies in the face of the prevailing image of Japanese food being subtle. It's a thick, savoury pancake stuffed with pork, squid, cabbage, cheese, *mochi* (pounded rice cake) – anything really (*okonomi* means 'as you like'; *yaki* means 'fry'). Once cooked, it's seasoned with *katsuo-bushi* (bonito flakes), shōyu (soy sauce), *ao-nori* (green laver), a tonkatsu sauce and mayonnaise.

Restaurants specialising in *okonomiyaki* have hotplates built into the tables or counters. Some places do the cooking for you; others give you a bowl of batter and fillings and leave you to it. (Don't panic: the staff will mime instructions and probably keep an eye on you to make sure no real disasters occur.)

Okonomiyaki is heavily associated with Osaka. Hiroshima has its own variety called *hiroshima-yaki*, where the pancake is thin (like a crepe) and the ingredients are layered rather than mixed. In Tokyo, *okonomiyaki* restaurants also serve *monja-yaki*, which has a very thin, runny batter.

gyū okonomiyaki · 牛お好み焼き
beef *okonomiyaki*

ika okonomiyaki · いかお好み焼き
squid *okonomiyaki*

mikkusu · ミックスお好み焼き
okonomiyaki with a mix of fillings,
including seafood, meat and
vegetables

modan-yaki · モダン焼き
okonomiyaki with yaki-soba and a
fried egg

negi-yaki · ネギ焼き
thin *okonomiyaki* with spring
onions

WAGASHI JAPANESE SWEETS

Sweets in Japan are traditionally considered an accompaniment for tea, though many restaurants have adopted the custom of dessert and end a meal with a serving of sliced fruit or maybe ice cream. Japanese confections are known generically as *wagashi* (as opposed to *yōgashi*, Western-style sweets such as cake and biscuits). The basic ingredients are just rice and a sweetened paste of red *azuki* beans (called *anko*). Flavour (usually subtle) and design (often exquisite) are influenced by the seasons. In spring they may be shaped like cherry blossoms or wrapped in cherry leaves; in autumn they might be golden-coloured, like the leaves, or flavoured with chestnut.

Okashi-ya (sweet shops) are easy to spot: they usually have open shopfronts with their wares laid out in wooden trays to entice passers-by. Buying sweets is simple – just point at what you want and indicate with your fingers how many you'd like.

anko · あんこ
sweet paste or jam made from *azuki* beans

kashiwa-mochi · 柏餅
pounded glutinous rice with a sweet filling, wrapped in an aromatic oak leaf

mochi · 餅
pounded rice cakes made of glutinous rice

wagashi · 和菓子
Japanese-style sweets

yōkan · ようかん
sweet red-bean jelly

Left: *Kaiseki* dishes **Bottom left:** *Sakura-mochi*, a rice cake with bean paste and pickled cherry blossom leaf

KAISEKI

Kaiseki is Japan's formal haute cuisine, where ingredients, preparation, setting and presentation come together to create a highly ritualised, aesthetically sophisticated dining experience. Key to *kaiseki* is peak seasonal freshness; as the ingredients should be at the height of their flavour, only subtle seasoning is used to enhance them. The table settings and garnishes, too, are chosen to complement the ingredients and evoke seasonality.

The meal is served in several small courses, which usually include sashimi (raw fish), something steamed, something grilled, and soup, and finishes with rice, then a simple dessert (though there may be many, many more courses). While fish is often served, meat never appears in traditional *kaiseki*. There may be a few different grades of courses (decided by the ingredients used, not the amount of food).

A good *kaiseki* dinner costs upwards of ¥10,000 per person; a cheaper option is to visit a *kaiseki* restaurant for lunch. Most places offer lunch menus featuring a sample of the food for around ¥4000. Alternatively, you can sample *kaiseki* by booking a night in a top-rate ryokan and asking for the breakfast/dinner option.

For the most authentic *kaiseki* experience, dine at a *ryōtei* (an especially elegant style of traditional restaurant) in Kyoto or Kanazawa – two cities known for their *kaiseki* culture. This is about as pricey as dining can get in Japan, ¥20,000 or more per person, with advance reservations required.

bento · 弁当
boxed meal with rice and several side dishes

kaiseki · 懐石
traditional Japanese haute cuisine

matsu · 松
extra-special course

take · 竹
special course

ume · 梅
regular course

NABE HOTPOT CUISINE

This must surely be the most convivial way of eating ever invented. The guests gather around the heavy metal pot suspended over a hearth, the beer and sake flow, the conversation never slows, and as the mixture begins to bubble and simmer, the room heats up, the host brings more beer, and an irresistible smell of slowly cooking stew begins to fill the room...

Nabe, the great winter warmer, is an age-old rustic style of cuisine and requires little preparation, and less washing up (unlike just about any other form of Japanese cuisine). There's almost no waste, the natural tastes of the ingredients are allowed to come through, and, as every Japanese impoverished student knows, the room gets heated as appetites get satisfied.

Cooking couldn't be any simpler. A basic stock, or in some cases just hot water, is placed in the *nabe*, then whatever ingredients are to hand are added, brought to a simmer, then guests fish out the vegetables, shellfish, fish or meat of their choice, dip them in a *tsukejiru* dipping sauce and... eat! The *tsukejiru* will most likely be ponzu, a mixture of dashi, *shōyu*, vinegar and yuzu.

Common *nabemono* (*nabe* dishes), include *chiri-nabe* (fish), *kani-suki* (crab), *dote-nabe* (miso and kaki oysters), *udon-suki* (udon, vegetables and shellfish), *botan-nabe* (wild boar), *ishikari-nabe* (Hokkaido salmon and vegetables) and *chanko-nabe* (the Sumo-wrestlers' miso or *shōyu* calorie-fest containing just about everything).

FUSION

In a sense, all Japanese cuisine is 'fusion cuisine'. Almost everything was imported at one time from neighbours China or Korea, or from South-east Asia, India, or even Europe and the US. Yet most has changed so profoundly as to be barely recognisable. Udon wheat noodles are a case in point. Wheat was imported from China via Korea as long ago as AD239, as were noodle-making techniques, but the Chinese don't eat udon, and the Korean version 'udong' tastes markedly different. Ramen noodles came from China, but have been so thoroughly adopted by the Japanese that the word 'ramen' is as often written in the hiragana script, used for native Japanese words, as it is in katakana, the script reserved for words of foreign origin.

Katsudon (deep fried pork cutlets served on a bowl of rice) is one of Japan's most common day-to-day 'fusion' dishes. The *katsu* part, the cutlet, was introduced from Europe in the 16th century, but it really became popular during the Meiji era when Japan reopened to the West, when it was served atop a *donburi* dish of boiled rice, accompanied with sliced *negi* (spring opinion), a well-beaten egg and dashi.

Pan (bread) is another borrowing from the Portuguese, and Japanese *pan-ya* (bakeries) stock unexpected sandwiches such as *an-pan* (bread stuffed with sweet red beans), *kare-pan* (bread containing curry) and the legendary *ichigo-sando* (a sandwich of strawberries and cream).

YOSHOKU / WESTERN FOOD

Left: *Katsudon*
Above left: *Katsu sando* **Above right:** gratin, but with a rice base

The Japanese adaptation of Western food, known as *yōshoku*, is not merely a side note to Japanese cuisine but an integral part. These dishes are as much a part of culinary culture in Japan as traditional dishes, such as soba noodles, tempura and sushi. Essentially, it is Western food that has been reinvented for the Japanese palate, and its origins date back to the Meiji period (1868–1912), when a century-long ban on eating meat was lifted and Japanese ports were opened. Travellers to Europe and the USA discovered different cuisines and adopted them back home. *Yōshoku* cuisine is typically found served at *kissaten* (casual chain diners), *famiresu* (family restaurants), some hotel restaurants and cafes.

KARE RAISU

Curry rice. Although curry originated in
India, this dish was first brought to Japan
by officers of the British Royal Navy in the
late 1800s. It's usually made with carrots,
potatoes and onions with a blend of spices
and includes meat or chicken. The curry is
then poured over white rice for a simple,
fast food.

OMU-RAISU

Taking its name from 'omelette' and 'rice',
this comfort food dish is an omelette
wrapped around fried rice and usually
drizzled with tomato sauce. The rice is
usually flavoured with beef stock and fried
with meat.

HAMBAAGU

As you might've guessed from the name,
this is a beef burger with a Japanese
twist. The *hambaagu* is a patty made with
minced beef, breadcrumbs, onion and
egg, cooked in a frying pan. It's not served
in a bread bun with cheese, lettuce and
tomato, but instead on a plate with rice,
salad and a choice of sauce.

DORIA

This dish looks similar to a gratin. It's a
baked casserole topped with creamy white
sauce, cheese and various other ingredients,
including chicken or seafood. It was created
in Japan by a Swiss chef in the 1930s.

THE SOCIAL HISTORY OF CURRY RICE

It is the cheap and cheery, can't-be-bothered-to-cook standby, a staple of winter school refectories, cut-price truckstops and shokudō (all-round, inexpensive restaraunts). Kare-raisu ('curry rice') prepared in seconds by adding hot water to an instant sweet, spicy roux, with vegetables or beef, added to rice, is ubiquitous. It is the choice of flu-ridden children, and anyone in need of homely, junk-food sustenance. It is barely recognisable to visiting Indians or Pakistanis as 'curry' at all.

The first time Japanese citizens encountered curry is carefully documented, in the diaries of a late-19th century Japanese sailor. In 1863, British warships were pounding Kagoshima into submission in retaliation for the murder of British citizen Charles Richardson by the Satsuma-han clan near Yokohama. Thirty-four Satsuma military officials were dispatched to France to lobby Napoleon lll for support. They left aboard the French warship Monsieur, and later changed to a postal vessel, where they witnessed Indian passengers cooking up what they described as 'aromatic mud'.

Not surprisingly, it didn't catch on, until Japan opened to the West, during the Meiji period, when it was added to the local staple, to form rice-curry. Its first creator may have been the Indian-born maid of a British trader. Others credit its invention, in 1876, to none other than US educator, scientist and entrepreneur, William Smith Clark, founder of the forerunner to Hokkaido University.

By 1906, it was being advertised as the perfect addition to miso soup, or as an accompaniment to 'Westernise' seaweed. A decade later, the 95th edition of the popular women's magazine Nyokan called it 'curry rice', and the name has stuck ever since. And in the 1930s, the modern, domestic curry rice industry was founded, aided and abetted by a new source of demand – the troops being shipped to fight wars in China. Over the next decade and a half it became used exclusively for military rations. After WWII, the instant curry rice, made by Hausu Shokuhin, became a nationwide success, and its popularity remains huge today.

SPECIAL DIETS

Restaurants in Japan are not as used to catering to dietary restrictions as their counterparts in some other countries, but they are slowly starting to get a bit better. Restaurants and inns that regularly host international guests are usually accommodating, as are restaurants in international hotels.

State your restrictions at the earliest possible opportunity, like when you are booking a ryokan. Given time, most places will try to be accommodating. That said, in many cases your options will be defined by how stringent you are about your restrictions; for example, unless explicitly noted otherwise, your vegetable tempura is going to be fried in the same oil as the prawns.

VEGETARIAN & VEGAN

On the surface, Japan would appear to be an easy place for veggies and vegans, but the devil is in the detail: many dishes (including miso soup) are seasoned with dashi, a broth made from fish.

Vegans and vegetarians will usually have options such as tofu and other bean products at a lot of restaurants, and many cities in Japan do have outlets that specifically offer vegetarian and vegan dishes. Happy Cow (www.happycow.net/asia/japan) is a good resource. In the countryside, you'll need to work a little bit harder and be prepared to explain what you can and cannot eat.

Of special note is *shōjin-ryōri*, the traditionally vegetarian cuisine of Buddhist monks; Kōya-san in Kansai is a good place for this.

HALAL

Japan now has more halal options than it used to have. For certified halal restaurants, see Halal Gourmet Japan (www.halalgourmet.jp).

ALLERGIES & GLUTEN FREE

Many chain restaurants and deli counters label their dishes with icons indicating potential allergens (such as dairy, eggs, peanuts, wheat and shellfish), but otherwise this can be tricky. You'll want to have a list of allergens written in Japanese on hand.

Gluten-free is particularly challenging, as there is little awareness of coeliac disease in Japan and

Below: *Otsu*, a noodle salad with tofu and coriander **Right:** Fresh produce on display in Kanazawa, Central Honshū

many kitchen staples, such as soy sauce, contain wheat (even restaurant staff may not be aware of this). The Gluten-Free Expats Japan! Facebook group is a good resource.

Anyone with an allergy to shellfish should be aware that Japanese dishes can contain shellfish in a dried and powdered form that is not easily detectable, though this is rare. If you are in doubt, ask '*Kairui haiteimasu ka?*' ('Does it contain shellfish?'). If the answer is '*hai*' (yes), desist. A traditional remedy for seafood allergy is to take juice of *shiso* (beefsteak plant).

There are a few individuals who are allergic to soba (buckwheat noodles). If you haven't had buckwheat before, just wait a moment or two before you take a second mouthful. The symptoms of soba allergy are instant, the same as a heavy asthma attack, and can be quite scary, but mercifully it's a rare condition. Gluten-free diners, however, can eat soba with impunity; buckwheat contains no gluten.

DIABETES

If you are diabetic, bring plenty of supplies and everything you will need, then pack some more. If you're travelling with a companion, it's a good idea to split your supplies between you in the event your luggage is lost. Medicine for diabetes called Tonyobyo is available in Japan, but getting it will be time-consuming and expensive, so it's best to come prepared.

© Westend61 / Getty Images; Alexander Spatari / Getty Images

JAPANESE STAPLES

Left: Sukiyaki in a traditional cast-iron pot

The cuisine of this teeming archipelago of over 6000 islands is a living part of its culture and is shaped by the staples that *washoku* (traditional Japanese food) is founded on; think soba, miso, sushi, dashi and rice. While food production and preparation techniques may have evolved – electric rice cookers arrived, agricultural machinery replaced back-breaking farming methods – the key ingredients that make up a modern Japanese meal have not changed dramatically over time. On average, rice consumption in Japan is declining due to changing diets, but it is still a crucial element in any Japanese meal. Overfishing is an increasing concern, and fish stocks are in trouble; yet sushi, sashimi and fresh seafood still dominate the Japanese diet. Mountain vegetables fill udon noodle bowls and are battered in light tempura as they have been for generations.

These main ingredients alone do not a Japanese meal make, though. A key element to any Japanese dish is the delicate balance and subtlety of flavour achieved with perhaps a dashi broth, a pinch of *shichimi togarashi* (seven-pepper spice), a sprinkling of *beni-shoga* (pickled ginger), a light touch of wasabi or a splash of *shōyu* (soy sauce).

It's this harmony of Japanese staples that tie together a cuisine that has been nourishing souls, warming bellies and bringing people together throughout history.

OKOME RICE

'Who could ever weary of moonlight nights and well-cooked rice?' —Japanese Proverb

The Japanese don't just consume *okome* (rice) all day, every day, they venerate it (and they used to pay taxes with it too). What's more, it's Japanese-produced rice or nothing: Oryza Sativa Japonica. To protect Japanese rice farmers, there are strict caps on the import of foreign rice, with imports carefully controlled.

Short-grained, translucent Japonica differs from its relatives *indica* and *javanica* in possessing amylopectin, the element that gives it its wonderful texture and slightly glutinous quality. The Japanese adore it to the tune of, on average, 54.4kg each per year. Yet their passion for it comes not merely from its taste – in the past, a meal was simply incomplete without the inclusion of *okome*. Though its consumption rate has lowered in recent decades, rice is the building block on which a Japanese meal is based, the core-helix at the heart of the Japanese culinary DNA. In its uncooked form it is called *okome*, the o- denoting respect, *kome* meaning rice. Cooked Japanese-style, it is called *gohan* – the *go-* prefix here the highest indicator of respect – denoting rice or meal (some, however, may use the more informal *meshi*, something akin to 'grub'), and when it is included in fusion cuisine and fast-food favourite, *yoshoku*, it is termed *raisu*. Such is its importance that when a Japanese person asks another if they've eaten, they ask *'Gohan wo tabemashita ka?'* ('Have you eaten rice?').

Yet rice's omnipresence in Japanese life is not merely a dietary or culinary convention; it has grown to have spiritual connotations as well. Even in ultra-modern Tokyo, a child will often be taught to scoop a small amount of white rice from the *suihanki* (electric rice cooker) to offer to the spirits of deceased ancestors in the family's *butsudan* (home altar), before heading to school carrying a lunch box filled with assorted bite-sized goodies – and, of course, some cooked rice.

90

TYPES OF RICE

Regional varieties of rice proliferate. The chardonnays and cab-savs of the Japanese rice world are the varieties *koshihikari* and *sasanishiki*, found throughout the archipelago, but especially renowned in Niigata, Fukui and Akita prefectures. The main types of rice include:

HAKUMAI OR JUBUZUKI

Daily white rice (often called sushi rice outside Japan), universally used in every dish from the humble lunch box to the finest *kaiseki* (formal cuisine).

GENMAI

The unpolished, unrefined, brown version is rarely spotted outside organic restaurants, as it lacks the fragrance and glow so desired of simple *hakumai*.

BLENDED RICE

Includes *shichibuzuki* (70% white, 30% brown), *gobuzuki* (50-50) and *sanbuzuki* (30% white, 70% brown).

MOCHIGOME

A glutinous version of regular rice, used to make the sticky *mochi* rice cakes served at New Year.

PREPARATION & CULTIVATION

Left: A farmer plants rice by hand **Right:** Rice fields in Kagawa Prefecture, Shikoku

which originally means steam) for 10 minutes, then the rice is ready.

Automation too has come to dominate the cultivation process, with the rural *minyo* (worksongs) and hours of backbreaking work replaced by the clank and clatter of rice planters and harvesters, whose studded metal wheels make them resemble spindly versions of WW1 weapons of destruction. Planting by hand is fast going the way of the *kamado*, but you may still see it in the deeply rural rice-producing areas, and in the crooked bent-over posture of the *Obaa-san* (grandmothers) who for decades toiled in the fields, where regional producers take their business as seriously as any French vineyard owner.

Traditionally rice was steamed in a large cauldron, set over an earthenware hearth fuelled with *maki* (wood choppings). This steaming process even has its own verb – *take* – which is used exclusively to describe rice preparation. Today, style has succumbed to convenience, and nearly every restaurant and private home relies on the electric *suihanki*. The rice grains are rinsed thoroughly in cold water, swished by hand in a circular scooping motion until the mix loses its cloudy appearance (this is essential). The rice is then placed in the *suihanki*: *hakumai* has an equal amount of water, while *genmai* has 50% more. Hit the button, and 20 to 30 convenient minutes later you have rice that is almost ready for serving. Let it sit (or *murasu* in Japanese,

Right: Edamame are salted green soybeans

OMAME BEANS

Given the country's Buddhist history, it's no surprise that Japanese cuisine has long-been dependent on this protein-rich food source as a vegetarian option for sustenance.

DAIZU

Top of the Japanese beanpile is indispensable *daizu*, the soybean (literally, 'big bean') that provides the raw material for such necessities as miso, *shōyu* (soy sauce), tofu, *yuba*, and the infamous *natto* (fermented soybeans). It also wends its way into such dishes as *hijiki-mame* (black spiky seaweed sautéed in oil, with soy and sugar) and *daizu no nimono* (soybeans cooked with seaweed and dried shitake mushrooms).

AZUKI

Azuki, the adzuki bean (written with the characters for 'little bean') used extensively in preparation of *wagashi*

NATTŌ

It's gooey, it's brown, it stinks, so what's to like about nattō? *These partially fermented soybeans, with the scent of ammonia mixed with foot odour, are the litmus test by which the Japanese judge a foreigner's sense of culinary adventure. Don't be surprised if someone asks you, 'Can you eat* nattō?'. *It is often served at ryokan breakfasts.*

Nattō is Japan's answer to Australian Vegemite or Sweden's Surströmming, but while it might not be everyone's cup of tea, this traditional food has been around for thousands of years and is being dubbed a 'superfood', said to offer health benefits ranging from improved cardiovascular health to stronger bones as it's loaded with vitamin K.

The most common way to eat nattō is by itself or as a topping on rice. If the taste is a little, ah, strong for you, try adding an egg on top or some ingredients to take the edge off, such as soy sauce or wasabi.

(Japanese sweets), often for the tea ceremony, and in the preparation of *seki-han* (red-bean rice) that the nation uses at times of celebration. *Bundo* is a small green *azuki*, and *kintoki* a large red variety, often cooked in sugar, named after its resemblance to the red-faced legendary child Kintarō – a hero from Japanese folklore who was believed to have superhuman strength.

SORA-MAME

The broadbean or broad horse bean, *sora-mame*, is often used in the same way as its Western counterpart: in a role as a savoury garnish, though again it is used in sweets. Other less common varieties are the *tora-mame* (the tiger bean, named for its stripes) and *hana-mame* (the flower bean, named after its beautiful blossom).

© Junichi Miyazaki / Lonely Planet

97

From left: *Wateishoku* (*ryokan* breakfast) tofu; Tofu is used in many Japanese dishes

TOFU

Tofu is one of Japan's most sublime creations, though the versions available in the West don't always varnish its reputation. Tofu is made by soaking dried soybeans, usually overnight, until they swell in size. They are then crushed and boiled to produce a foamy liquid, which is then cooked over a low heat before being strained to get the soy milk and lees. The soy milk is solidified into blocks, known as tofu. If you get up with the larks and head down to your local tofu maker for post-dawn *kumiage-dofu*, the still-warm, freshly made, creamy tofu melts in your mouth. Another classic way to eat tofu is as *hiyayakko*, cold blocks of tofu covered with soy, grated ginger and finely sliced *negi* (spring onion), a favourite on izakaya menus.

As always, the freshest dipping ingredients make the finest dish.

YUBA

Yuba *(soy milk skin) is a staple of* shojin ryori *(vegetarian temple cuisine) and a speciality of Kyoto. It is a marvellous accompaniment to sake when it is served fresh with grated* wasabi *and* shōyu tsuyu *(soy sauce vinegar). Dekitate-yuba, the just-made stuff, is best. Its creation is a time and labour-intensive process in which* tonyu *(soy milk) is allowed to curdle over a low heat and then is plucked from the surface using either chopsticks or equipment especially designed for the process. Don't worry, you can buy it pre-packed. A dried form is added to soups.*

TYPES OF TOFU & DISHES

Kinugoshi Soft, silken tofu. Mainly used in soups, especially miso.

Momen Firm tofu. Usually eaten by itself, fried in *agedashi-dofu*, or used in the Kyoto classic *nabe* hotpot dish, *yudofu*.

Agedashi-dofu An izakaya menu staple: deep-fried tofu, served in a hot fish-broth sauce, usually topped with ginger, grated daikon and a little spring onion.

O-age Thinly sliced especially thick tofu traditionally fried in *goma-abura* (sesame oil). It is a key ingredient in the celebratory *chirashi-zushi*, and in *inari-zushi*, named after the fox-deity and rice-god that protects shrines throughout the country, the most notable being Fushimi-Inari Taisha in Kyoto.

Koya-dofu The monks of Koya-san Buddhist temple in Nara make their own distinctive greyish, thick *koya-dofu*, always served cold. It was reputedly first made by Buddhist patriarch Kukai in the 9th century, who freeze-dried the tofu outdoors on a clear winter night.

> *Both* momen *and* kinugoshi *take their names from the technique when the hot soy milk is strained – if the material used is cotton, the resulting firm tofu is* momen; *when silk is used, it's* kinugoshi.

MISO

A precursor of miso arrived on the Japanese mainland from China sometime around 600AD, not long after Buddhism, and its inhabitants have been gargling it down ever since; at lunch, dinner and even breakfast. Made by mixing steamed soybeans with *koji* (a fermenting agent made from either barley, soybeans or rice, that works in a way somewhat akin to yeast) and salt, miso is integral to any Japanese meal, where it is most likely to be present as *miso-shiru* (miso soup) or as *dengaku* (a flavouring), where it is spread on vegetables such as eggplant, and *konnyaku* (devil's tongue).

Miso soup is made of a mixture of dashi stock and miso, and shellfish such as *shijimi* (freshwater clams) or *asari* (short-necked clams); assorted vegetables such as daikon, carrot or *gobo* (burdock; especially good for the digestion); pork in *tonjiru*; or simply tofu. In preparation, it should never boil, and is often served with a *suikuchi* or topping of sliced *negi*, spring onion, or *mitsuba* (trefoil). Good *shijimi* miso soup combined with the aromatic pepper sansho is a heavenly combination, and it's rumoured to be good for your liver if you happen to indulge in too much sake.

REGIONAL VARIATIONS OF MISO

One of the great delights of touring Japan is to sample miso's regional variations. Some would argue that you can recognise a person's birthplace by their choice of miso.

Sendai-miso The dizzyingly salty *sendai-miso* of rural Miyagi prefecture is a country creation. A gorgeous ruddy brown, it matures with age.

Shinshu-miso From Nagano prefecture in the Central Alps; less wild and less salty, though it is still unmistakably rustic, with a much-praised slightly tart quality.

Edo-miso Named after the former capital before it became Tokyo; it's dark, fiery red, slightly sweet, and as forthright and unpretentious as the Edokko Tokyo-ites who are its chief consumers.

Hatcho-miso Has its own much-told history. Originally created in Okazaki, Aichi prefecture, not far from Nagoya, it was first made in the Hatcho area (8th district) of the town, where it continues to be produced. It was shipped to Tokyo (then Edo) by the ruling elite family, the Tokugawa, who came from the Okazaki area and were sorely proud of their home-grown product (the secret of which they'd kept under wraps for some time). The Edokko were hugely underwhelmed, shipped it back, and developed their own.

Kyoto Shiro Miso A delicate, sweet, aristocratic white miso that inhabits the rarefied world of *Kyo-ryori* – Kyoto specialist cuisine. In particular it is used in making *ozoni*, a miso soup containing *mochi* (pounded rice cakes).

TYPES OF MISO

Kome-miso The most common type, made from rice.

Mame-miso Made from soy beans, most common along the Tokai coastline of Honshu.

Mugi-miso A barley miso popular throughout Kyūsh (except in Fukuoka, where they too make *kome-miso*).

SHŌYU: SOY SAUCE

From the lacquerware tables of Kyoto's *ryōtei* exclusive restaurants, to the grease-embedded counter of the corner ramen shop, *shōyu* is ubiquitous. Surprisingly, it's a relatively new addition to Japanese cuisine. Although a primitive form of *shōyu*, hishiyo was made by mixing salt and fish in the Yayoi period (300BC–300AD); *shōyu* in its current form only dates back to the Muromachi era (1333–1568). It only achieved widespread popularity somewhere between 1603 and 1867 in the Edo period, when it was first exported.

Its 20th century mass production made a household name (and multimillionaires) out of the brand Kikkoman, but *shōyu* is still made, using traditional methods, at small companies throughout the country. The importance of soy sauce lies not merely in its use as a condiment – it is integral to many cooking and pickling processes, and the *tsuyu* sauce or dipping sauce is the linchpin of Japanese noodle cuisine. Just to prove its worth, *shōyu* has its own deity: Iwaka-Mutsukari-no-Mikoto (God, by extension, of Japanese cooking) enshrined at Takabe-jinja in Chikura cho, Chiba Prefecture.

TYPES OF SHŌYU

Koikuchi-shōyu The dark-brown 'thicker taste'. Widely used for a variety of applications, especially in the Kanto region around Tokyo. It is perfect for teriyaki cooking (but can't be used for soup).

Usukuchi-shōyu The chestnut-coloured 'thinner', much saltier variety (sweetened and lightened by the addition of mirin). An aromatic favourite of the Kansai region, it is best suited to clear soups and white fish. It is especially important in enhancing the colour of a dish's ingredients.

REGIONAL VARIATIONS OF SHŌYU

Tamari-shōyu Thick and wheat-free (it contains only soybeans and salt), was once the *shōyu* made in rural homes, now comparatively rare. It is generally made in Central Honshu, particularly in Fukushima prefecture, and is used mostly with sashimi and in making the sauce for *unagi no kabayaki* (grilled eel).

Shottsuru A striking soy sauce made from fish in Akita Prefecture; almost resembles Vietnamese *nuoc mam.*

MIRIN

Generally referred to as 'sweetened sake', though it isn't, is the liquid formed from a mash of glutinous rice mixed with malted rice and *shōchū*. Mirin is used extensively in Japanese cuisine. Primarily it is used as a sweetening agent, being 10 times sweeter than sake, and preferred over sugar, as the inclusion of mirin adds a quality of depth to dashi and sauces. It contains around 13% to 14% alcohol, though this is often largely burned off prior to use, especially in *sunomono* (vinegared dishes) and *aemono* (dressed salads), whereupon it is called *nikiri-mirin*. Mirin was once served as an alternative to sake, and the good stuff, usually called *hon-mirin*, is still sold in sake shops today. If you fancy a swig, Japan's smoothest, classiest *mirin* is rural Aichi prefecture's *mukashijikomi*.

Clockwise from top: *Izumo* soba, made from whole buckwheat; Tonkotsu ramen, a Kyushu speciality; *Shippoku*-style soba

MEN/MENRUi: NOODLES

Japan must be the only country in the world where museums dedicated to noodles are must-visit attractions and every last citizen is a certifiable noodle-nut. The phrase 'menrui amari suki ja nai' ('I'm not too keen on noodles') is one you'll rarely hear. Everyone has a favourite restaurant (preferably unknown to anyone else, an anaba, a 'cave-place'), a favourite dish, a favourite stock (of great antiquity and Masonic secrecy), even a favourite convenience-store variety. And the hype is justified. Japan's noodles know no equal in quality, subtlety, presentation and sheer style.

SOBA BUCKWHEAT NOODLES

Soba's popularity arose not with its delicate aroma or distinctive, subtle, elegant-but-earthy taste, but with its ability to deter that terrible connoisseur bugbear – starvation. Buckwheat grows excellently in thin mountain soils where nothing else will, and, with its rapid 75-day passage from seed to grain, it made an excellent back-up whenever the rice crop failed. It is also packed with nutrients, protein and vitamins C, B and E.

Soba noodles are traditionally sliced by hand, to make *teuchi-soba*, but as the dough easily breaks when stretched after kneading, it is often either sliced by machine or, in the case of *teuchi*, *tsunagi* (a binding agent) is added, usually wheat flour. A ratio of 20% wheat flour to 80% soba is said to produce the finest results, though some purists swear by the dark, 100% soba, *juwari*. Soba noodles are a light brown-grey in colour and the width resembles spaghetti.

Purist and train station noodle-stand gobblers alike take their soba in one of two ways, hot or cold. The obvious seasonal preferences apply, but cold soba always carries a slightly pretentious air – if you order plain, cold soba with a cold dipping sauce, *zaru-soba*, it half-implies you mean business.

Hot soba comes in a bowl containing *tsuyu* (a hot broth consisting of *shōyu*, mirin, sugar and *dashi* stock). Cold soba comes on a *zaru* (bamboo grid tray) to be dipped in separate cold, stronger *tsuyu*. You add to the *tsuyu* ingredients such as grated daikon (radish), *sarashi-negi* (sliced spring onion), *tororo* (pounded *yama-imo*), *katsuobushi* (bonito flakes), yuzu (the wonderfully fragrant Japanese citron), and, ubiquitously, wasabi.

OTHER POPULAR SOBA DISHES

Mori-soba Like *zaru-soba* but with dried nori seaweed; always the priciest.

Tenzaru *Zaru-soba* with tempura, usually prawn, with its own separate tempura *tsuyu*.

Tempura-soba Served hot, featuring tempura.

Kamonanban & Torinanban Served hot, featuring duck and chicken respectively, with sliced *negi*.

Sansai-soba The exquisite soba dish, where mountain vegetables perfectly complement a delicate broth and the subtle buckwheat flavour.

Adding a final touch to the proceedings are the condiments, usually *sanshō* (the gorgeously aromatic, aniseed-like Japanese pepper) and *shichimi* (the red spicy blend of seven peppers).

UDON/SOMEN: WHITE WHEAT NOODLES

Udon is made from *kyoriki-ko* (strong wheat flour mixed with salt and water). It's kneaded well, stretched and sliced. Another arrival from China (in the Nara period, 710–794), it was long a staple.

Today, the white wheat noodles are found nationwide in forms either fat, thin, round or flat. One popular regional variation is Nagoya's flat *kishimen* served in that region in a miso broth. Kanto's version of *kishimen* is *himokawa*, a slightly wider version. On the island of Shikoku, Tokushima's famed *sanuki-udon* is often sold at self-service restaurants, where the customer steams their own noodles and dips them in the *tsuyu* (dipping sauce), with ingredients of their own choosing. They must be the most egalitarian of noodles.

As with soba, udon is served hot with *tsuyu* or cold without.

Kama-age-udon A popular version where hot noodles are dipped into a cold *tsuyu* (its equivalent actually exists in soba, *seiro-soba*).

Hiyashi-udon & Bukkake-udon Other favourites are simple cold *hiyashi-udon* and *bukkake-don*, where cold *tsuyu* is splashed on the udon itself.

Nabeyaki-udon A hotpot-style mix of shrimp and vegetables.

Misonikomi-udon Like *nabeyaki*, but with a miso broth.

Kizami-kitsune In the Kanto area, udon with unsweetened fried tofu is called *kizami-kitsune* or *tanuki-udon*; with sweetened fried tofu it is a *ma-kitsune*. In Kansai, the latter only is served, where it's called *kitsune-udon*.

Left: *Sanuki-udon*
Right: A chef preparing
kamatama (egg) udon

SOMEN

*A close relative of udon is the
wonderful summer noodle,
somen. Also made from wheat
mixed with salt and water, it
contains* goma-abura *(sesame
oil), thus despite its 'lightweight'
refreshing image, it is quite high
in calories. It is always hung
to dry in sunlight, one of the
Japan summer's most evocative
late-afternoon sights. Miwa
village in Nara is the* somen *hub,
producing a very thin noodle,*
Miwa-somen *with similar
regional variations in Kawachi,
South Osaka and the island
of Shodoshima in the Inland
Sea. The thinnest noodles are
called* Ito-somen, *while Tochigi
Prefecture's Nikko produces a fat
version,* Nikko-somen.

*While other ingredients are
rarely mixed into udon dough,
somen often has additions such
as green tea,* cha-somen, *egg
yolk,* kimi-somen, *shrimp in ebi-
somen and the starch-like kudzu
in* kuzu-somen.

©Junichi Miyazaki / Lonely Planet

RAMEN

Ramen is Japan's great national dish. Chances are high that you will see it being slurped on a daily basis by the Japanese at some time or another. 'Ramen' is an amalgam of the Chinese word meaning 'to stretch' and the Japanese suffix for noodles, '-men'. The stuff's popularity is enormous, with ramen shops galore, instant ramen noodles now a multibillion yen business, and itinerant ramen *yatai* (street vendors) a picturesque and welcome nocturnal stop-off in all major big cities. Fukuoka in Kyūshū is especially famous for these.

At the heart of good (and bad) ramen is the dashi or stock, made intrinsically from either *torigara* (chicken bones) or *tonkotsu* (pork bones), with the addition of either vegetables, *shōyu* or miso. Ramen chefs closely guard the secrecy of ingredients and their precise ratios, though most stick within these basics. A chef wishing to create a subtle, delicate (adjectives not often heard describing ramen) stock may use the expensive dried fish, such as *urume*, used in udon stock preparation. *As'sari* refers to a light, less greasy stock, *kotteri* to a thick, grease-laden, garlicky version.

The noodles are made from wheat flour mixed with egg and, present in most ramen, *kansui* (alkaline water). The noodles are kneaded, left to sit, then stretched with both hands. Curly noodles, in a Taiwanese style are called *chijirimen*, and should you like your ramen 'al dente', make sure to specify you'd like *katame*.

Until recently, ramen was also referred to as *chuka-soba*, especially in Western Japan, though the term tended to imply less use of *kansui*. Now *chuka-soba* has become a kind of sub-genre, suggesting ramen in a lighter, almost always *shōyu*-based dashi.

TYPES of RAMEN

Ramen types fit into four basic categories, each with a distinctive origin: shōyu ramen, from Tokyo; shio ramen and miso ramen from Sapporo; and tonkotsu, white pork broth ramen, from Kyūshū, especially Hakata in Fukuoka. Recent upstart additions are Onomichi ramen from Hiroshima prefecture, Kitakata ramen from Fukushima prefecture and Wakayama ramen, from, you guessed, Wakayama prefecture.

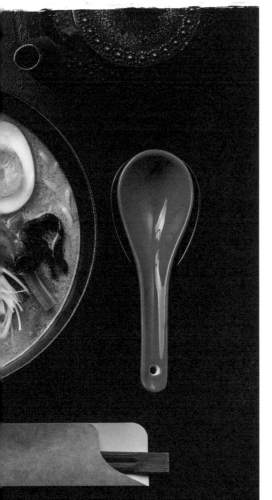

© Lisovskaya / Getty Images

RAMEN NOODLE TOPPINGS

The noodles are served in hot soup, with toppings such as:

Char siu (sliced pork);
Moyashi (bean sprouts);
Shinachiku (pickled Chinese bean sprouts);
Negi (sliced spring onions);
Naruto (white fishcake with a pink, whirlpool-shaped inset) ;
Nori (dried seaweed).

With tonkotsu, expect **ki-kurage** (cloud-ear fungus; 'tree jellyfish'), **yudetamago** (boiled egg) and **beni-shoga** (red pickled ginger).

SEAFOOD

Japan's historical dependency on the sea is nowhere better illustrated than in its use of fish, and shellfish, with sometimes damaging results to local fisheries as the demand outweighed considerations of maintaining stock. The good news is that Japan's emphasis on regional specialisation means that local communities are aware of the need to preserve what resources remain.

© Japan Online Media Center

OVERFISHING & REGULATIONS

Japan's fishing industry has gone into serious decline in recent years, after once being home to the world's largest catches. The main causes for the decline are habitat loss, increased industry competition and, most significantly, overfishing. Overfishing has long been an ecological issue for Japan, and the government has only recently started to take serious measures to curb the problem.

Japan did attempt to set catch limits for decades, though these limits were well beyond levels considered to be sustainable outside of the country; the justification for this was to protect the livelihood of local fishing communities. But, as the fishing stocks continued to plummet, the Japanese government has introduced more serious cap limits. In 2016, limits were set for the prized bluefin tuna weighing less than 30kg. Despite this, many continued to overfish, so harsher penalties were introduced and cap limits were adjusted to include larger bluefin tuna, also. As of 2018, fishers were required to submit reports on their Pacific bluefin tuna hauls, and any Japanese fisher who is caught violating these restrictions will face up to three years in jail or a 2 million yen fine.

Left: Karato Market, Yamaguchi

SUSHI

Sushi is vinegared rice, accompanied by vegetables, seafood and sometimes other ingredients, such as egg or exotic fruits. The practice of making sushi originated hundreds of years ago as a way to make fish last longer: the vinegar in the rice acted to ferment the fish. Nowadays, without the necessity of preserving ingredients, it tends to be served as a fast-food option with fresh fish, and eaten with fingers, not chopsticks, even in formal settings.

SASHIMI: RAW FISH

O-sashimi or *otsukuri*, as it's called in Kansai, is thinly sliced raw fish, and is a key component in Japanese formal cuisine, not least in *kaiseki-ryori*. It is also a regular on sushi-shop menus, and it's eaten in the home as a small luxury. Freshness is paramount.

More often, sashimi is simply arranged, with garnishes typical of the season, on an elegant porcelain dish. You dip the fish, perhaps wrapped in *aojiso* (green beefsteak plant), into strong *shōyu* (often *tamari-joyu*) that contains wasabi and *benitade* (water pepper, a dark red peppery garnish). Even ordinary fish deserves the best *shōyu* and freshly grated wasabi.

POPULAR TYPES of SASHIMI

Maguro (tuna) *Akami* is the most common and is the deep red loins of the fish. The pink, fatty belly meat is called *toro*.
Shake (salmon) As with tuna, often you will also find salmon *toro* – the fatty, buttery belly meat.
Tai (sea bream)
Tara (cod)
Tako (octopus) Can be eaten raw but is commonly poached first, too.
Ika (squid)

Sashimi is not solely used to refer to fish. Thinly sliced raw meat a la carpaccio is also given the term, as in Kumamoto's speciality ba-sashi, *an abbreviation of* ba-sashimi, *raw horse meat.*

JAPAN'S MOST POPULAR FISH

© Ming-Hsiang Chuang / Shutterstock

Fish is a Japanese staple. It's eaten as a main dish in a bento box or at a restaurant, cooked at home, sliced raw and eaten as sashimi and delicately placed on top of rice in sushi. Not only is fresh-caught fish eaten in huge quantities but fish is also an important ingredient when dried and processed, such as *katsuo-bushi* (dried bonito flakes used in stocks and broth).

TUNA

Buri (Yellowtail or amberjack) weighs up to 15kg and is especially good as sashimi, grilled, or served as teriyaki. Best in autumn and winter, its younger cultivated form is called hamachi. It is eaten at New Year in Western Japan, first as sashimi, then added to *ozone*, a miso soup containing *mochi* (pounded rice cakes). Pacific bluefin tuna is a prized catch and a popular choice for sushi and sashimi, but it is increasingly under threat of overfishing.

Related to the tuna family, bonito or skipjack tuna is an important player in Japanese cuisine. *Katsuobushi* form the main ingredient of dashi stock.

Left: Tuna at a market
Right: Plated fugu

© KPG_Payless / Shutterstock

MACKEREL

The Hokke Atka mackerel became popularised during WWII as a cheap source of protein. This grey fish with light brown stripe, caught off Hokkaido and Northern Honshu from winter through to spring, has a high fat content. It is best grilled, especially with a teriyaki sauce, deep fried, or served as *nimono* (a simmered dish).

Saba, the Pacific mackerel, is a beautiful, mother-of-pearl hued fish. It is the key ingredient in sushi and in the Kochi speciality *saba-no-sugatazushi* (mackerel sushi roll). Found throughout Japan; it's best in autumn.

Aji (horse mackerel) is taken all year and is most prolific in West Japan from spring to June, in East Japan from May to July, and it is used as sashimi, *shioyaki* (grilled) and *netsuke* (simmered).

SALMON

Shake (or *sake*), also known as the dog salmon, is a large fish reaching a length of up to 1m. River salmon are best in October. High-seas salmon is best eaten from early May to late June. Most *shake* is salted as *shiozake*, and grilled, used in *nabemono* (stew) or steamed with sake as *sakamushi*. It's also used in sushi.

SEA BREAM

Tai (sea bream) is a very popular fish in Japan. *Madai* is considered the best, and is in demand for weddings. Peach-red in colour, plentiful in the Sea of Japan and Inland Sea (but scarce on the Pacific side), it reaches 100cm in length. It's used in sashimi and in Wandane clear soup.

PUFFERFISH

Famed for its expense, and deadly propensities, the fugu (pufferfish or blowfish) comes in several varieties, and is most famously caught in Western Honshu's Shimonoseki, or Kita-kyushu from late autumn to February. When the Nanohana safflower blooms, it is called Natane-fugu, *indicating the end of the season, when it is tastiest and most poisonous.* Tora fugu, *the 'tiger fugu', is preferred, and is used as sashimi and in* nabemono, *known as* chirinabe. *The sashimi tessa is sliced so thinly one can see the design on the porcelain dish beneath. Just enough of the poison is left in the fish to slightly numb one's tongue.* Fugu-shirako *is also a sake accompaniment, and the pufferfish's toasted fins are served in* hirezake (*hot sake*) *as a part of fugu cuisine.*

SARDINES

Iwashi (dried sardines) is not just a cheap lunch. It is the Clark Kent of Japanese cuisine, always ready to transform into a culinary Superman. Its true nature is revealed in its role as a key ingredient in that most fundamental item of Japanese food – dashi. Discover a great, clear, deep, light stock, and the chances are that it's a humble sardine at work. *Katakuchi-iwashi* and *hibinago* are especially good. And that's not all. Poke a branch of the *hiiragi* (holly tree) into a sardine's head, stick it outside your house, and it's a talisman to dispel evil. This superstition dates back to the Heian period.

Below: Preparing *menme yu-ni* (braised whole fish wrapped in kombu)

© Junichi Miyazaki / Lonely Planet

KAISO: SEAWEED

Seaweed forms an important part of the Japanese diet and is an integral part of its cuisine.

Wakame *is found throughout the country, although Tokushima's is considered best, and it is harvested from May to June. Since the Nara period, its anti-aging properties have been recognised, a fact reflected in its name which means 'young woman'. The fresh version is used in sunomono, suimono, and in dashi. Dried* wakame *is also commonly used:* shioboshi-wakame *(dried in saltwater),* ran-boshi *(dried unpretentiously on the nearest beach) or* shio-nuki-wakame *(washed only in plain water, no salt, and dried).*

Nori *is best known in its dried and toasted form as the outer layer of* norimaki *sushi. Small sheets of* yakinori *are used to scoop up rice mixed with raw egg in a typical ryokan breakfast. It is often added to soba and ramen dishes (mainly in Kanto), mixed with salt and sesame for use in* furikake *(a savoury topping sprinkled on plain white rice), and is an ingredient in* shichimi togarashi *spice.*

Kombu *(kelp) has a role in Japanese cooking that cannot be underestimated, as it is a key ingredient in dashi. Ma-konbu, growing to almost 2m in length, is harvested from Hokkaido's Uchiura Bay.*

Hijiki *is a dark black, spiky looking but actually soft seaweed. It is especially good sautéed in shōyu with soybeans in a dish called* hijiki-mame. *Taken from Japan's Pacific coast, as with* konbu, *it has been proven to prevent hardening of the arteries. What's more, it strengthens teeth, is good for babies' bones in utero, and is economical.*

DASHI: BASIC STOCK

A great dashi is essential for great Japanese cuisine, as it is the crucial element in soups, *tsuyu* (dipping sauces), *nimono* and *nabemono*, and for cooking fish and vegetables. Typically it is made from either *katsuo* (dried bonito) or kombu (kelp seaweed). Its role in enhancing the flavour of food is paramount, and good chefs guard the precise details of their dashi ingredients with a zest bordering on paranoia. Stocks may also be made with shitake mushrooms, shellfish or small fish.

Dried bonito is easy to spot in a Japanese market. It is the thing which looks least like fish – it is more like a piece of driftwood. The Japanese have been drying *katsuo* since ancient times, when the summer fish was dried to preserve it through the winter season.

Superstition attaches itself to the humble bonito in several ways. It is still a common gift at New Year and is given to teething babies; tradition says they will develop perfect teeth. More often, though, it is grated either by hand for dashi using a plane (exactly the same as a carpenter's plane) into a *kezuri-bako* (specially designed box), or by machine in the marketplace. Ready shaved *katsuobushi* is convenient, but markedly less tasty.

Kombu was first harvested in Japan around the 6th or 7th century, when it was an early export to China, but it was not until a thousand years later that the black, shiny *ma-konbu* began to be collected in earnest on the southern and eastern shores of Hokkaido. Its dashi became instantly succesful in the Kansai region, and in particular in Kyoto, where it appealed to the Buddhist chefs preparing *shojin-ryori* (strictly vegetarian temple-cuisine) for both its health-giving properties and its suitability for use with tofu.

Both stocks are prepared in the same way. The water containing the ingredients is brought to a brisk boil, then the heat is immediately turned off. The flakes slowly sink to the bottom of the pan, and the liquid is filtered through a muslin sieve. It is important not to squeeze the *katsuo* or else the stock will become bitter. When making a soba buckwheat *tsuyu*, however, a slight amount of bitterness is considered a desirable element.

Left: Octopus may be served in vinegar or in balls
Right: Steaming seafood

KAIRUI: SHELLFISH & MOLLUSCS

Sazae (horned turbo) is served in its shell either pot-grilled or raw as part of a sashimi platter. The *wata* (organs) are bitter but also eaten.

Awabi (abalone) are a transgendered shellfish, simultaneously male and female, best eaten as sashimi. It is a typical summer delicacy in high class ryotei or sushi shops.

Asari (short-necked clam) is beautifully patterned, yellow, red or purple, and best from winter to early spring. It is used in miso soup and *nabe*.

Bai/baigai (a type of whelk) is 7cm in height and especially good from Toyama Bay.

Ebi (prawn or shrimp) is a term used to refer to any number of sea or river-dwelling edible 10-legged crustaceans. Larger specimens (up to 20cm) are grilled and fried, in the popular *ebi-furai*, but the smaller ones are used in tempura and as sashimi.

Hamaguri (Venus clam) has occupied an important role in Japan's culinary history (it was the first shellfish ever eaten). It's a spring speciality is caught on the Northern coast west of Hokuriku, and in Tokyo Bay, Ise Bay, the Seto Inland Sea, and the Ariake Sea. *Hamaguri* need to be washed well, and are often grilled with yuzu (citrus).

Hotategai (scallop) is served grilled or as sashimi.

Igai/Murugai (mussel) are used mainly in miso soup and as *shōyu-yaki*, grilled with *shōyu*.

OTHERS

Ika (squid) is a major component in Japanese cuisine, and comes in around 100 edible varieties. The most popular is *surume-ika* used, not surprisingly, to make *surume*, dried squid (it's a chicken-and-egg deal regarding its name). Squid can be found grilled on izakaya menus and in sushi.

Tako (octopus) varieties include the Seto Inland Sea's *ma-dako*, best in January and February; the large *mizu-dako*, most often taken in Hokkaido; and small *li-dako*. Octopus is never served raw, even in sushi where it appears thickly chopped as *tako-butsu*. It is eaten with vinegar, as *nimono*, and in the Osaka perennial favourite *tako-yaki* (octopus balls).

Kani: (crabs, lobsters & freshwater crabs) are high on the list of winter favourites, especially in Hokkaido. They are usually cooked in *nabemono* with vegetables, boiled and steamed. *Kegani* (horsehair crab) is the common nickname for the *O-okuri-gani* ('giant chestnut crab') famous in Hokkaido.

UNAGI: EEL

Unagi (eel) is most auspiciously eaten during the dog days of summer, especially on a day corresponding to the water-buffalo in the Chinese zodiac '*doyo no ushi no hi*', when it is said to convey vigour. Famously, *unagi* are sliced down the back in Kanto, and down the belly in Kansai, further proof that these two regions belong to different culinary universes.

Anago (conger eel) translates as 'The Child of the Hole', from its nocturnal underwater habitat. **Ma-anago**, caught throughout Japan, is the best tasting.

Kuro-anago (a black bodied eel), the largest of the species, growing up to 1m in length, is mainly used in Kamaboko and is found in Southern waters. The **Gin-anago** is a short, overweight version.

Long ago *unagi* was grilled on a skewer. More popular now is the charcoal-grilled *kaba-yaki*, which takes its name from its colour, reminiscent of the *kaba* birch tree, and is served in a teriyaki sauce. It is also often served as a *donburi*-dish, *una-don,* which in Kansai is called *mamushi*, after its resemblance to the Japanese pit viper.

WHAT'S IN A NAME?

The Japanese character for **Ayu** (sweetfish) consists of two elements, *sakana* (fish) and *uranai* (meaning 'fortune-telling'). This bizarre nomenclature originates in Japan's distant past when the Empress Kogou, en route for (Sankan) Korea, was focused on two of Japan's long-standing pastimes: angling and invading Korea. She caught *ayu* on Tamashima, in Matsu'ura, and decided this was auspicious, and Korea would be defeated. History doesn't record whether the fortune-telling fish was right. *Ayu* feed on freshwater algae, and retain their smell when not gutted; atypically, they cost more when bought ungutted, because true epicures make their entrails into *shio-kara* (that's fermented viscera for novices). Thus it is also called *kogyo*, the aromatic fish.

The Japanese word for **aji**, (horse mackerel) combines *sakana* (fish) and *san* (the word for 'three'), indicating that it was traditionally caught in the third month, March. As *aji* is also a homonym for 'taste', it has long been held in high esteem.

Shake (salmon) is usually termed *shirozake* ('white sake'), because of its white meat, although in Hokkaido it is called *Aki-aji*. Most Japanese assume this comes from the phrase for 'red-taste', after the colour of the salmon flesh. However, it really originates from the indigenous Ainu name, *Akiachip*.

Tai (sea bream) has long been regarded as Japan's finest, most auspicious fish. Its high rank in the world of Japanese cuisine is reinforced by a play on words, *Omedetai* meaning, loosely, the 'wish-to-congratulate fish', hence its presence – symbolic or real – at wedding ceremonies.

In Akita and Hokkaido, if they don't eat **hatahata** (sandfish) it's still not winter. Its name incorporates *sakana* (fish) and *kaminari* (thunder), therefore in Akita it's called *kaminari-uo* (lightning fish), as during the spawning season thunderstorms regularly appear.

The origin of the word **unagi** (eel) is delightfully improbable. It comes from a combination of the 'U' of *ushou* (cormorant-fisher), and *nangi* (meaning difficult, in the sense of slippery and difficult to catch). U plus *Nangi* equals unagi. Mmm...

SEASONAL CALENDAR OF FISH

SUMMER

Extremely tasty but scary-looking *hamo* (pike conger), with their sharp mouths and teeth like a hacksaw blade, are best in summer. Caught in Kansai, especially in Kyoto and Osaka.

Kanto dwellers will shun *bera* (wrasse), but this fish is a Kansai favourite, especially the *kyusen* or *sasanoha bera*, good for *shioyaki*, *nitsuke*, and best in early summer to autumn. Taken in the southern part of Chubu, *hata*, another early summer-to-autumn fish, is used in sashimi, and is also good for *nitsuke*.

WINTER

On the world endangered species list, *tara* (cod) translates as 'the snow fish', after its white belly.

Taken north of Sendai in the east, and north of Tottori Prefecture in the west, it is best in winter. For sashimi, it must be extremely fresh, otherwise it is good in *nabemono*.

SPRING

Katsuo appear in January and February in the warm Ogasawara islands, riding the warm Kuroshio current up to the Sanriku-oki islands (Aomori) from August to September.

In autumn they finally reach Southern Hokkaido, and then turn back south towards the mainland of Honshu. These large *kudari-gatsuo* (descending bonito) have the finest tasting meat, best of all in May. Most of the catch however goes into *katsuobushi*, for use in dashi.

Japanese anglers' best-loved river fish are the *iwana*, *yamame*, and *ayu*. The *iwana* inhabits the narrow, upper reaches of mountainous clear rivers, followed by *yamame* where the river widens, and then the deepest-water dwelling *ayu*.

The *iwana char* (literally, 'rock-fish', after the boulder-strewn riverscapes it inhabits) is found only in Hokkaido, Honshu and Shikoku. As tasty as *yamame*, it is best in late-spring and early summer. It is fantastic as *shioyaki*, served with *sansho*.

Tai (sea bream) is another popular fish best in early spring.

Famed for its ability to predict earthquakes – not kidding, the nation's top seismology labs all keep 'em – the fresh water namazu (catfish) is best in winter, when it is used in nabemono. It is bewhiskered, and rather jovial looking.

YASAI/ SANSAI: VEGETABLES

Japanese vegetables largely fall into two categories: *sansai* and *yasai*. *Sansai* literally means 'mountain vegetables', implying vegetables gathered from the wild, as opposed to *yasai* (cultivated vegetables), though some *sansai* are grown, and some *yasai* grow wild, so the terms are not strictly exclusive. *Sansai* are most commonly served as tempura, *aemono*, *nimono*, *tsukemono* and *sunomono*. They are also present in the soba-shop standard, the very tasty *sansai* soba.

© tdub303 / Lonely Planet

128

SANSAI VEGETABLES

Fuki-no-to The unopened butterbur bud; a spring addition to miso soup.

Seri Water dropwort is most often used in soups and with *sukiyaki*.

Udo Resembles asparagus.

Zenmai & Warabi *Zenmai* (royal fern) and *warabi* (bracken) look ominously triffid-like, but are tasty staples of *sansai* cuisine.

Yomogi Mugwort is combined with *mochi* or udon, imparting an unnerving dark green colour to both. It is also a traditional medicine.

Junsai Water shield is another Japanese once-tasted-never-forgotten experience. Its leafy shoots, gathered from the surface of rivers in spring and early summer, are encased in a gelatinous cover far too reminiscent of frog-spawn. *Junsai* is added to *suimono* (clear soups). It is expensive and nigh on tasteless. You pay for the weird sensation as it slips down your throat.

YASAI VEGETABLES

Shungiku Edible chrysanthemum leaf originated in Europe. A spring vegetable commonly used with *sukiyaki*, it is very strong tasting and should be boiled once and soaked in cold water before use.

Mitsuba Trefoil found in Japan and China; grows in damp places in early spring, and is oft-used as a topping for miso soup, or in the steamed savoury-custard dish, *chawanmushi*.

Edamame Japan's most visible green beans. These 'branch beans' are served in the pod, as an izakaya accompaniment to beer, especially in the summer. The pods are dusted in salt, which transfers to the beans as you pop them in your mouth between swigs of foamy ale.

Daikon The giant white radish is an important daily vegetable, served in a variety of ways. As *oroshi-daikon*, it is grated finely as an addition to noodle dishes – it is said to aid digestion.

Konnyaku Devil's tongue, or elephant foot, is made into cakes or is coated with miso as *dengaku*. Thinly sliced, it is *shirataki*, the gelatinous bootlace lookalike in *sukiyaki*, or in slightly fatter bootlace form it is *ito-konnyaku*, a common addition to *nabemono*.

Shoga Ginger, though not used as widely as in other parts of Asia, is often used grated as *oroshi-shoga* to flavour dipping sauces or to put on tofu. It is pickled as *beni-shoga* and used as an addition or accompaniment to sushi dishes, and is also added to soups and stocks, and is the main flavouring in thick soba and udon dishes.

Take-no-ko Bamboo shoots arrived in Japan, in Kagoshima, in the 16th century from China, and are extensively used in *nimono* or soups, or added to rice as *take-no-ko-gohan*.

Negi Welsh onion, or *cibol*, is very widely used, primarily as a *nabe* or soup ingredient, and as an addition to *tsuyu* (dipping sauces) for noodles.

DAIKON

Daikon serves another unique purpose: apprentice chefs are forced to learn how to peel it in a single unbroken strip, a process known as katsuramuki, *so as to master knife technique – and patience. Once the daikon is peeled, the outer skin is finely sliced to serve as* sashimi no tsuma, *or* sashimi no ken, *the white, background mount for raw fish.*

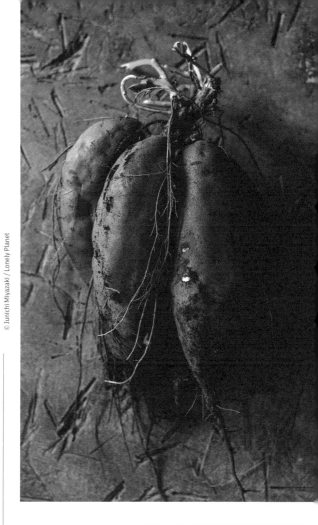

© Junichi Miyazaki / Lonely Planet

Gobo Edible burdock must be immediately placed in vinegar water after cutting to remove bitterness, whereafter it is boiled in vinegar water or *togijiru*, the water left over after rinsing rice. *Gobo* makes a fantastic addition to soups as it produces an excellent, deep, natural dashi.

Nasu Eggplants, used in popular *nimono*, *agemono* and tempura dishes, are perfect with miso, most notably in *nasu-dengaku*. Naturally sweet, Japanese eggplants do not need to be salted prior to cooking. A lush purple colour indicates freshness.

Renkon Lotus root, best from winter to early spring, has strong connections with Buddhist cuisine through its webbed, wheel-like cross-section reminiscent of the 'wheel of reincarnation'. In season from winter to early spring, it has to be boiled with vinegar to remove its strong iron content that otherwise turns it black. It is served in *sunomono*, *nimono*, and tempura, especially as *karashi-renkon*, in which the gaps between the 'spokes' are filled with Japanese mustard.

SATSUMA—IMO: SWEET POTATO

A common sight and sound in even small Japanese cities is the yaki-imo, roast sweet-potato vendor, who usually does the rounds in a small, open-backed truck, on which a charcoal stove is roasting the potatoes. The smell is irresistible, not least if you've just stumbled out of a pre-dawn karaoke session. Sweet potatoes don't just feature in savoury dishes – they are also widely used in sweets in Japan.

Right: Wild mushrooms
are added to a hotpot in
Nagano Prefecture

KINOKO: MUSHROOMS

Japan's humid climate makes it a mycologist's fantasy, with over 4000 species of mushroom and fungus (about the same as in all Europe), many edible. They are all generally used in the same way, in miso soup, as tempura, mixed with rice as *kinoko-gohan*, or in *nabemono*. Only *matsutake*, the Cadillac of the Japanese mushroom world, is served in a unique manner.

Shiitake Strong tasting, and easily cultivated; they are used to make vegetarian-friendly dashi.

Maitake Translates as 'dancing mushrooms', from the waving, arm-like shape of their branches; wonderful,

gentle and earthy – one of Japan's great tastes. They go well with both creamy, Western-style sauces and Japanese *shōyu* or miso-based soups.

Shimeji Small, white-stemmed mushrooms most commonly served in miso soup; their larger cousins, *hon-shimeji*, are considered something of a delicacy.

Enoki-dake Quite odd-looking, with long thin white fungal stems topped with a creamy-white cap. They resemble early *Lost-in-Space*-ish alien lifeforms, but they're great lightly blanched in salads, sautéed in butter, or in miso soup; best from November to March. Alas, wild enoki are rather scarce.

Matsutake, or **mat'take** for short, are monumentally expensive. A single small example, found wild in Japan, will sell for anywhere between ¥25,000 to ¥45,000, depending on the region. Mat'take are prized for their fragrance even more than their rather delicate taste, and are most often served steamed in a small 'teapot'. You savour the aroma from the pot, and drink the juice in which the mat'take has been steamed from a small porcelain cup. You then eat the mushrooms themselves. Mat'take can be grilled in foil, or steamed with rice to make mat'take-gohan. All are an autumn feature of rural ryokan inns.

Part of the reason for their expense is that mat'take are near impossible to rear artificially. Imports from Korea, Australia, New Zealand and the USA are cheaper, but considered pale imitations of the real mat'take.

KTSUKEMONO: PICKLES

As an accompaniment to boiled rice, pickles are present in most Japanese meals. They are also important accompaniments to sake and beer.

Pickles are named for the ingredient – mostly vegetables, but also fish, the length of time pickled, and the pickling base, usually either miso, salt, vinegar or *nuka* (a paste made of rice bran). The latter was once considered such an important part of household life that daughters would include it in their wedding dowry, and *nukamisozuke* (pickles which have been kneaded into a mixture of miso and *nuka* and left to mature – sometimes through an entire winter), are unique to Japan.

Shiozuke is pickling in salt, an overnight process for *asazuke* (lightly pickled vegetables) or for much longer for *umeboshi* (pickled sour plums).

GARNISHES

WASABI JAPANESE HORSERADISH

Fresh wasabi, especially the naturally cultivated variety from the pure streams of alpine Nagano prefecture, is sublime, one of the great tastes of Japanese cuisine. The real stuff suffuses gently through your mouth. It is both pungent and smooth. In combination with good *shōyu* or noodle *tsuyu* (dipping sauce), it is truly memorable.

SANSHO

Yet another remarkable ingredient in Japanese cuisine. Zanthoxylum *sansho* is its Sunday name, and the leaves or the pod rather than the seed are used for aromatic flavouring. *Sansho* has a splendid taste, something akin to lemony aniseed. It goes perfectly with white fish, *unagi*, udon and *nabe*.

SHISO PERILLA, BEEF-STEAK PLANT

A member of the mint family Lamiaceae, but with a certain pungency and hint of basil. This remarkable aromatic, nettle-shaped leaf can be used as an accompaniment to sashimi and sushi, and is used in soups and in tempura. As its name suggests, it is a good accompaniment to beef. In fusion dishes, it often accompanies or replaces sweet basil.

SHICHIMI TOGARASHI

This popular condiment for noodle dishes and *nabemono*, translates as the 'seven taste pepper'.

YUZU

Japanese yuzu is a marvellously aromatic citrus fruit, usually whitish-yellow or green.

SU VINEGAR

Japan's first vinegar, *umezu*, came as a result of salt-pickling plums. It is used much as Western-style vinegars, and especially in *sunomono*.

135

NIKU: MEAT

GYŪ-NIKU: BEEF

After the Meiji-period emperor's 1873 'repealing' of the Buddhist prohibition against the killing of sentient creatures, beef eating suddenly became the rage. It was civilised, chic, cheap and good. The Age of Beef was ushered in. Since then, the Japanese have indulged in everything from *shabu-shabu* to teriyaki burgers.

Wagyu This Japanese beef has cult status both in Japan and abroad, thanks to its rich marbling, which makes for very melty, tender meat. Most Wagyu comes from a breed of cattle known as Japanese Black. Within that category, there are a few premium brands that hew to strict quality control and are prized as top-grade meat. These include Kōbe, Matsusaka and Ōmi.

Kōbe, Matsusaka and Ōmi are all named for places that have naturally become pilgrimage spots for keen carnivores, though high-grade Wagyu can be enjoyed in any major Japanese city. Brand-name beef comes with pedigree but it doesn't come cheap (prices start around ¥5000 for a small lunch portion and rise steadily from there). Two things to keep in mind: as the meat is very rich, often a small portion will do. Also, any non-brand Wagyu with a rating of A4 or, even better, A5 is going to be top-notch (and probably cheaper).

Often the meat is seared at high temperature on a *teppan* (steel hotplate), diced and served with rice and miso soup. You can also grill strips of Wagyu over

coals at Korean barbecue-style places called *yakiniku*; eat it *sukiyaki* or *shabu-shabu* style; or order it at steakhouses paired with wine. All mention of premium Japanese beef comes with the following disclaimer: eat this, and you'll be spoiled for life.

Kōbe-gyū Kōbe is known worldwide for its top-class beef, considered by many to be the best in the world. Highly marbled, it's naturally tender and rich in flavour. It's also held to very strict regulations. To be accredited as *Kōbe-gyū* (Kōbe beef), the meat must fulfill certain criteria for marbling, colour and texture; crucially, it must also come from a Tajima breed of Japanese Black born, raised and slaughtered in Kōbe's home prefecture, Hyōgo. There's a widespread belief that the cows are massaged, fed beer and played soothing music, though the Kōbe Beef Marketing & Distribution Promotion Association disavows it. There are many places in the city to try it, though note that it is very expensive, especially for the best cuts (which really give you a taste for that famous marbling). Splurge on the cut rather than the size; the fat content makes Kōbe beef very filling.

Matsuzaka-gyū The slightly less well-known, but equally expensive Mie prefecture counterpart, or Shiga's Ohmi-gyu. The Tajima region is famed for its Tajima-gyu veal. A slice of top-class Japanese beef is quite marvellous to behold, its marbling a delta-like network of fine, white strands, set against a luscious deep red flesh. Equally dizzying is the bill.

Hida-gyū Hida's culinary fame rests in *Hida-gyū* (Hida beef). Hida beef is fast becoming a serious competitor for Japan's best beef and is considered by many to be the ideal Wagyu. The cows are raised in the mountaineous region of the Gifu prefecture and Hida beef has a higher amount of fat marbling, *shimofuri*, which gives it its distinctive juiciness and tenderness.

BUTA-NIKU: PORK

Eaten in Japan since the Edo period, the Yorkshire, Berkshire and Hampshire breeds are preferred. In Okinawa, the ears are a delicacy – you might have to spit out the hair. In Kyushu, the carcass is prized for its role in tonkotsu (pork broth). More generally, however, it is eaten as tonkatsu, pork cutlets, in pork shabu-shabu, or served on rice as katsudon.

INOSHISHI/SHIKA: WILD BOAR & VENISON

The meat-hungry Buddhists of the Nara period were in a quandary. With the recent prohibition against eating four-legged creatures, they came up with the novel idea of turning a ferocious but now sacrosanct mountain-dwelling boar into a very edible, Buddhist-Kosher sea-mammal. Thus the *inoshishi* (wild boar) became the *yama-kujira* (mountain 'whale'), a species we know some Japanese have few qualms about offing. Astonishingly, nobody batted an eyelid at this blatant, bald-faced piece of semantic subterfuge.

So today, *inoshishi* is most often used in *botan-nabe*, its strong smell lessened by being stewed in miso. Kumogahata in Kyoto, Sasayama in Hyogo, Asakuma-yama in Ehime, and Izu's Amagi-yama are famed for their boar cuisine, which is best from November to March.

There is a long-standing taboo against eating *shika-niku* (venison), as the deer is traditionally considered a messenger of the gods. That is why Nara's temples and shrines are famously surrounded by the wandering beasts. That said, non-believer rural hunters have long taken deer (the male of the species only); its best season is autumn, when the light-tasting red meat is served as sashimi or in *nabemono*.

© Tom-Kichi / Getty Images

Above: A Japanese wild boar
Right: Yakitori at a street stall

NIWA-TORI/ TORI-NIKU: CHICKEN

Chicken was already being eaten in the Nara period. Probably the first examples were arrivals from China, kashiwa (yellow chicken). The bird makes up roughly a third of Japan's meat consumption.

UMA *Hardly eaten outside Yamanashi, Nagano and Kumamoto prefectures, uma (horse meat) is most often found raw as basashi, or in nabemono, when it is generally called sakura-niku 'cherry meat' or ketobashi. Mare's meat is said to be best.*

There are some notably excellent regional varieties. You've heard of the chicken that laid the golden egg, but the egg that produced the Golden Chicken must have come from Akita prefecture's outrageously expensive thoroughbred, *hinai-dori*. Nearly as pricey, but not quite is Nagoya's *cochin*.

Chicken are roasted whole (*maruyaki*), steamed (*mushi-dori*), fried (*kara-age*, also known as *tatsuta-age*), and minced as t*ori-minchi* (which is often made into *tsukune*: chicken balls). It can be served raw, thinly-sliced as sashimi, is excellent with a ponzu dipping sauce, or made into *tori-wasa*, blanched in boiling water *yubiki*, and served as *aemono*, with grated wasabi. Western visitors often appreciate it in the izakaya and street-food staple yakitori (grilled chicken on skewers).

© tkyszk / shutterstock

JAPANESE DRINKS

J apan has a long history of – and love for – drinking, and not simply for the pure, hedonistic fun of it, though the Japanese are no slouches at partying. Alcohol is the great social lubricant that sets the Japanese free of the intricate web of social and familial obligations that hounds them from cradle to grave. It gives them a valid excuse to shed themselves of society's rules for a moment and have a good time. And they do. This 'let's party' determination finds hard-working salarymen and women hitting the drinks hard at after-work parties, and it's not uncommon to see office workers in suits passed out and slouched on the ground at train platforms, attempting to get home.

Though a lot of Japanese people love to drink, many struggle with the ability to handle their alcohol. Japanese scientists attribute this to a deficiency in ALDH (E2), a component of the aldehyde dehydrogenation enzyme that aids the processing of alcohol, which is said to afflict around 40% of the population. However, alcohol doesn't seem to fuel aggression or violence in Japan

Left: Sake bottles in a shop

like it can do in many Western countries. It is fairly unusual to meet obnoxious drunks here. Drinking in Japan is mostly fun.

One of the country's signature drinks is *nihonshū* (sake; 'the drink of Japan'), which has existed for as long as history has been recorded in Japan (and odds are a lot longer). It plays an important part in a variety of Shintō rituals, including wedding ceremonies, and many Shintō shrines display huge barrels of sake in front of their halls. If sake's not your thing, there is also an ever-expanding, strong craft-beer scene and, of course, award-winning whisky to get excited about.

Teetotallers, fear not. It's not only an alcoholic tipple that plays an important part in Japanese society; this is a nation with a strong tea-drinking culture – particularly *o-cha* (green tea) – and the country is as packed with cafes and teahouses as it is bars and clubs. If you want to really get to know Japanese tea, visit a teahouse or speciality shop, which will usually serve matcha. The culture of drinking this high-grade powdered form of green tea entered Japan along with Zen Buddhism in the 12th century, and matcha plays a crucial role as the tea used in the revered art of the tea ceremony.

Though tea is the historical drink of choice, *kōhī* (coffee) has been drunk in Japan for a long time, and in recent years third-wave coffee has moved into the main towns and cities of Japan in a big way. Not only is it a welcome addition for foreigners looking for a decent caffeine hit, but many of Japan's trendsetters are selecting a meticulously brewed single-orgin coffee as their favourite hot beverage.

Whether it's sipping sake at a stand-up bar or savouring a bowl of matcha while admiring a temple garden, there is no shortage of ways to socialize and, at the same time, appreciate the culture of Japan over a few drinks.

TEA

Tea is enjoyed in ornate ceremonies and everyday canteens across the country. It's a refreshing and deeply Japanese drink, as well as an expression of creative harmony.

GREEN TEA: O-CHA

Japan's love affair with green tea dates back to its introduction from China. The Chinese Buddhists had long appreciated the role of a good cuppa in preventing one from nodding off during prayers. Yet no one can really agree when tea was introduced to Japan. Some suggest the Nara period (710-794), while another source credits the introduction to Buddhist saint Dengyo Daishi in 805.

In the 12th century the monk Eisai introduced the Rinzai school of Zen Buddhism to Japan. He also brought back both Chinese tea and the Chinese tea ceremony, a move that saw the drink really take off. Tea became as popular as Zen. At the end of the 12th century, green tea was sowed at Uji, near Kyoto – still producing some of the best tea in Japan– and the Japanese court and aristocracy took wholeheartedly to tea, and its formalised ritual drinking: the tea ceremony. It took another half a millennium or so

© 7maru / Getty Images; HMS / AWL

THE TEA CEREMONY IS NOTHING MORE THAN BOILING WATER, STEEPING TEA, AND DRINKING IT

SEN NO RIKYU, 16TH–CENTURY TEA MASTER

for the rank and file to pick up the habit, its popularity spurred on by the invention of a convenient, newfangled form – sencha – leaf tea. Since then, the Japanese have become well and truly tea-struck, enjoying a cuppa anywhere from in exquisite teahouses purpose-built for the job to factory canteens and convenience stores.

The powdered form used in tea ceremonies is called matcha. Unlike the usual infusion style of tea, matcha is whisked into an emulsion and drunk unstrained. However, the common tea of choice is *bancha*, a course tea, always drunk hot, and often served free of charge in restaurants. It is drunk to quench the thirst, is cheap, and is made from larger, older tea leaves and may include stems. When it is roasted (the magnificent smell that pervades every Japanese shopping arcade) it becomes *hoji-cha* (roasted tea), which possesses a deep, wonderfully smoky taste, has the lowest level of caffeine, and is

good hot or cold. When roasted and popped rice is added to *bancha*, it becomes *genmai-cha*, which possesses a nutty, less-smoky quality.

The leafy green sencha (infused tea), is served to be enjoyed in its own right. It is made from leaves that are reasonably tender and young, and is often served on special(ish) occasions. When the real top brass stop by, however, out comes the *gyokuro*, a magnificently fragrant, umami-rich, comparatively rare tea that is grown in specially constructed bamboo cages that shut out much of the early spring light, resulting in extremely tender leaves that are only picked in a single harvest. No surprise, then, that it can be expensive.

The TEA CEREMONY: SADO/CHANOYU

Sado (the Way of Tea) has influenced art, calligraphy, poetry and cooking. A ceremony offers the chance to appreciate its rules and rhythms, and pause for a good chat.

No-one can dispute the influence of *sado* (the Way of Tea) or *chanoyu*, (tea's hot water) on Japan's spiritual, artistic, and cultural heritage. Born from Zen Buddhist meditative precepts, and popularised by Japan's warrior-class, tea has created some of Japan's most spectacular works of art. It brought about the gardens and teahouses of Kyoto, that city's incomparable raku (ceramic teaware), its calligraphy, its poetry; indeed, even Japan's most refined cuisine itself, *kaiseki* – all owe their existence to, and are informed by, the Way of Tea.

Sado incorporates the delicately rigorous aesthetic of *wabi-sabi* (the unadorned purity of natural imperfection) fused with a relaxed and peaceful satisfac-

tion in being solitary. It demands awareness of and sensitivity to nature, and the changing of the seasons; a spiritual, meditative, reflective quality; and a socialising role of equanimous meeting, symbolised by the teahouse design, with its *nijiriguchi* (low entrances that require each participant to lower their head in humility upon entering). Ceramics selected for tea ceremonies were often dented, misshapen or rough in texture, with drips of glaze running down the edges – and all the more prized for it. The most famous styles associated with the tea ceremony are raku, *shigaraki* and *bizen*.

There is an amalgam of complexity and simplicity to a tea ceremony, and an understated but very real discipline. The mechanics, overtly at least, are none too complex, though difficult for the beginner to master. And even more difficult for the experienced practitioner to refine. A tea ceremony can, in fact, be an informal affair among friends. A traditional tea ceremony, however, must be infused with *wakeiseijaku* – harmony, respect, quiet and solitude.

A full-on *chaji* (tea ceremony) goes something like this. The guests, usually clad in kimono,

assemble in a waiting room, select a member to act as the main guest, then proceed to the garden, and the *tsukubai* (stone trough) from which they ladle water to hand to mouth to purify themselves of worldly concerns.

They then enter the teahouse, admire the calligraphy work in the *tokonoma* (recess) and greet the host. Expect a light *kaiseki* meal, sake, and a *wagashi* (Japanese sweet) to offset the bitterness of the thick, green matcha tea that is to follow.

Guests retire to the garden or the waiting room, then re-enter the tearoom, stopping to admire the flower arrangement that has replaced the hanging scroll in the *tokonoma* (alcove in a house).

The thick *koicha* (opaque matcha) is passed in a single bowl from the host to the guest,

who savours its strong bitter taste, which slowly overcomes the sweetness of the *wagashi*, before wiping the bowl and passing it to the next person. Talk is of, what else, the tea – is it from Uji or Shizuoka or elsewhere? What is its poetic name?

The host then rebuilds the coals in the brazier, and prepares the thinner *usucha*, which he or she whips to a frothy consistency with the bamboo *chasen* (tea whisk), and passes to each person. This too is drunk, there's more talk of the utensils, the lacquer of the container – perhaps it's a fine example of *Wajima-nuri*, from Ishikawa prefecture – and the fine crafted curve of the tea scoop. Cultured conversation reigns. Then the guests depart, and the outside world seeps in. The *chaji* is over.

TEA KAISEKI: CHA-KAISEKI

Cha-kaiseki creators are part chefs, part artists. Their goal is to produce a stylised banquet that combines rice, soup, sashimi, grilled dishes and seafood, and sets you up perfectly for the tea drinking that follows.

Kaiseki, or more specifically *cha-kaiseki* (tea *kaiseki*), is a quintessential Japanese style of eating. It is seasonal to the nth degree, and its true practitioners are part-chef, part-visual artist. Its greatest adepts are found, where else, but in Kyoto.

The tea ceremony meal begins with *shiro-go-han* (white rice), *miso-shiru* (miso soup) served in a lacquerware bowl and *mukozuke* (a sashimi dish) or *sunomono* (vegetables marinated in vinegar) placed on the far side of the tray.

Chopsticks made of cedar are used and sake is served in a Kannabe ironware pitcher. *Nimono* (stew or simmered dishes) are served in lacquerware bowls, often so hot that it is difficult to remove the lid. *Yakimono* (grilled or pan-fried dishes) are served on ceramic plates, with additional rice and soup.

In the *hashiarai*, or chopstick-washing, *kosuimono* (a clear broth soup) is served to clear the palate – and to clean the chopsticks, hence the name.

During the third and final course, *hassun*, the host is served *yamanomono* (mountain dishes) and *uminomono* (seafood) by the guests. Pickled vegetables, in this context called *konomono*, are also served with browned rice in salted water.

KŌHĪ: COFFEE

Despite the strong tea-drinking culture, the Japanese do drink *kōhī* (coffee). Chain cafes such as Doutor, Tully's and Starbucks (a nonsmoking oasis with free wifi) dot the country, but historically coffee was only drunk in retro *kissaten* (coffee shops). These are family operations where the coffee comes served in small, delicate cups accompanied by little pitchers of cream. Staff might be wearing black bow ties, possibly jazz is filling the air, and the decor harks back to the '50s and '60s. They have a charming old-school ambience to them,

which contemporary cafes just can't match.

If your coffee needs lean more toward a modern offering, there is no problem finding a well-made flat white, a cold-drip filter or a nitro brew – Japan can certainly deliver with its speciality roasters and brewers (some local, some expat businesses); this is where you're more likely to see a younger, more edgy crowd. While the third-wave coffee movement has gained more and more popularity throughout the country, it has meant, unfortunately, that the number of *kissat-*

en is in decline. Coffee-loving visitors to Japan should try to seek out a *kissaten* during their stay; it offers a peek into history and times gone by, plus the coffee is usually very well-crafted.

Japan is also the perfect place if you're looking to add to your home coffee-making paraphernalia. High-quality craftsmanship and design are available with well-known equipment icons, such as Hario V60 pourover and the Kono Dripper, which was produced by Coffee Syphon and established in 1925.

SOFUTO DORINKU: SOFT DRINKS

The archipelago that long resisted Western invasion has lost its battle with the likes of Coca-Cola and Pepsi (helped not a little by its own conglomerates, Suntory and Kirin). Yet there are a few homespun drinks that catch the eye.

First and foremost is Ramune, invented back in 1872, a hugely sweet, lemonade concoction, that comes in a Victorian-style bottle, complete with a marble in its crimped neck that can be notoriously tricky to open. It is sold at summer festivals, in shopping arcades, and on the approaches to major shrines and temples. For the Japanese, it is the taste of nostalgia, of a time when things were scarcer, times harder, but pleasures simpler.

Another throwback is the startlingly-titled Calpis, a Nyusankin or lacto-bacillus sweet concoction said to have been inspired by the Mongolian fermented horse milk drink, *airag*. Another lacto-bacillus breakfast favourite is the equally sweet Yakult, which is now well-known around the world. In Japan, it's delivered door-to-door by representatives akin to Avon sellers, driving refrigerated mopeds.

A popular sports drink is the equally bizarrely named but beloved Pocari-Sweat, which claims to replenish ions (electrolytes) in the body.

151

JiDOHANBAIKi: VENDiNG MACHiNES

Japan has the highest number of vending machines per capita in the world: more than 5 million machines. These legendary contraptions are everywhere. Really, everywhere. On Mount Fuji. In funeral homes. On trains and ferries. One definition of deeply rural Inaka countryside is 'the place without vending machines'.

Vending machines sell everything from fresh flowers and books to individually wrapped melons. But you'll see drinks machines most, stocked with everything from water and sports drinks to beer, iced tea and hot and cold cans of coffee.

The oldest surviving vending machine in Japan is a wooden-stamp selling machine, which is on display at the Postal Museum on the 9th floor of Tokyo's SkyTree Town. The machines really gained popularity in the '70s, spurred on by the novelty of having the technology to be able to serve hot and cold drinks.

Critics believe they are environmental disasters – guzzling power 24 hours a day – and toxic nightmares, yet they are irresistibly convenient. You can grab a can of beer, a cup of sake, a bowl of ramen noodles, and a hot or cold coffee for a handful of loose change. They offer convenience for the busy Japanese, and also offer a bit of privacy and avoidance of having to feel embarrassed about going into a store to buy certain products, such as condoms, feminine hygiene products, toilet paper and even nappies (diapers).

HOW DO THEY WORK?

For visitors to Japan, it couldn't be easier getting your piping hot, milky coffee or ice cold barley tea or Pocari Sweat (a popular local sports drink) from one of these vending machines; you don't need to read Japanese and they're easy to comprehend. Most machines accept coins between 10 yen and 500 yen, and some accept 1000-yen bills. Cold drinks have a blue label, hot drinks have a red label. In the past, you could find alcohol vending machines on every street corner, but they are becoming hard to find these days; you may have more chance in rural areas. Some now have an ID-checking system installed.

ALCOHOLIC DRINKS

BIRU: BEER

The Japanese love *biru* (beer) and drinking it is an essential part of the culture. It's also the perfect antidote to those sweltering humid summer evenings, when most of the population seems to retreat to a hotel rooftop beer garden, to sink icy steins of lager beneath lanterns emblazoned with Sapporo or Kirin.

Beer is served either in bottles *bin biru*, or as draft *nama biru* ('living beer'), which comes in frosted, handled *joki* (glasses) in large, medium or small sizes (*dai-joki*, *chu-joki* and *sho-joki*). Often these are abbreviated to *dai*, *chu* and *sho*, and it's quite acceptable for a parched customer to yell '*nama dai chodai*!' (something like 'Give us a big draft!'). Beer gardens and izakaya are not places to stand on ceremony. Party groups often get a *picha* – a pitcher of beer to share.

Beer first hit Japan around 400 years ago, courtesy of Dutch traders. Then came the Norwegian William Copeland – Norwegian by way of the US – who opened the country's first brewery in Yokohama in 1868, having studied brewing in Germany and the US. There's no record of why Copeland felt the urge to up sticks and traverse the globe to set up a beer-making concern, but it was an astute move. The Japanese

had already tasted beer imported from Britain and Holland to the treaty ports of Yokohama, Nagasaki and Hakodate, and the upper classes in particular took to the stuff, which appeared oh-so modern and Western.

Copeland was no slouch at business either. He quickly picked up on the new invention, pasteurisation, and a year after its founder had published his dissertation, Copeland's Spring Valley Brewery was employing the technique – and thus selling gallon upon gallon of beer. In the late 19th century, the three breweries – Kirin, Asahi and Sapporo – that now dominate the Japanese beer trade came into being; later on Suntory was added to the mix.

Today, the production of

jibiru (local beer) is on the rise, yet it's the big breweries that still have the beer market sewn up. Japan had a strict alcohol tax law that restricted brewing to the four large breweries; this was relaxed in 1994, allowing smaller operators to brew beer. Since then, a craft-beer scene has been constantly evolving and new, independent craft brewers keep popping up around the country, yet it's still a tough market to thrive in. For true beer lovers, the mainstream Kirins, Asahis, and Sapporos are disappointingly similar – nearly all are pale lagers using light malts and moderate hop content. Though in recent years, they have branched out to make different or seasonal beers in the style of the craft-beer world.

SAKE WA HYAKU YAKU NO CHO
ALCOHOL'S the BEST of a HUNDRED MEDICINES

JAPANESE SAYING

155

Clockwise from left: Drinking beer in an izakaya; Beers at Coedo Brewery; Pouring craft beer; Kyoto Brewing Co bottles its saison beer

The BEST of JAPA

© Tony Chen @brewfulllife Brewery

© Kyoto brewing Co.

© Minoh Brewery

HOKKAIDO

Japan's northernmost island is something of a local craft-beer leader, not to mention the home-land of Sapporo. Based in the city of Otaru, Hokkaido Brewing is a craft brewer that does eclectic fruit beers – from a pear ale to a yuzu (Japanese citrus) lager – and some traditional ales.

KYOTO

The Kyoto Brewing Co, set up by a Welshman, an American and a Canadian, brews Belgian- and American-inspired beers at its brewery and taphouse, not too far from Kyoto Station.

OSAKA

Minoh Brewery, a female-run brewery, is an Osaka institution and has been a vital part of the craft-beer scene since 1997. Its award-winning core beers include a double IPA, a pale ale, a weizen, a pilsner and a stout, along with creative seasonal offerings.

NESE CRAFT BEER

© Yasuko Aoki / Getty Images

© Hitachino Nest

© Coedo Brewery

NiiGATA

Beers are produced using the famous, pure underflow water from the Agano River in northwest Japan at the well-respected Swan Lake Brewery, around since 1997. Some of the beers it produces use local *koshihikari* rice in the brewing process, too.

IBARAKI

Originally a sake brewer since 1823, Kiuchi Brewing produces the well-known line of Hitachino Nest beers, now found around the world. Beers are aged in *shōchū* casks. Some feature yuzu and red rice in the ingredients.

SAiTAMA

Coedo Brewery started off as an organic farming company before transitioning into beer, and now exports its product globally. It is famous for its Coedo Beniaka, an unfiltered amber ale using roasted *kintoki* (sweet potatoes), a speciality of the Kawagoe region.

SAKE: O—SAKE/ NIHONSHU

From the first visit to a Shintō shrine at one-month-old, *Omiya-mairi*, to the *O-soshiki* Buddhist funeral rites, the Japanese are accompanied by sake. Its place in religious life comes from its associations with rice – the food of the gods – and its symbolic purity, and it is consumed, often in large quantities, at every major rite-of-passage event in a Japanese person's life. In the Shintō wedding ritual, the bride and groom seal the marriage by exchanging sake cups and drinking sake, *sansankudo no sakazuki*, which invokes the gods to intervene to help the couple, and through the sharing of sake, come closer together and create a bond of friendship. Sake is offered to the family *butsudan* (the altar that houses the spirits of one's departed ancestors), and at family graves during the mid-summer O-bon festival commerating ancestors, when the spirits are thought to return to this world. It is proffered to the roadside Buddha statues that dot the countryside, and is a feature both ritually symbolic and

Right: Sake barrels
in Okinawa

SAKE by DAYLIGHT is CRUEL

SAKE BY TWILIGHT IS MELLOW

SAKE at MIDNIGHT INTOXICATES

SAKE at DAWN ENTRANCES

WRITER FUJIMOTO GIICHI'S
PRECEPTS FOR DRINKERS

earthily practical, at every *matsuri* (festival).

Precisely when the art of brewing reached Japanese shores is lost in the mists of time. Tradition ascribes its introduction to emigrants from Korea, about the end of the 3rd century, who no doubt learned the technique from their omniscient neighbour China, where they had been knocking back a fermented rice drink since time immemorial. The Kojiki (Record of Ancient Things), however, adds 200 years to that estimate. The general populace started brewing sake in the 12th century, and by the end of the 15th, the districts of Itami in Osaka and Ikeda in Hyogo had established their superiority, a position which, together with the city of Nishinomiya and Kyoto's Fushimi district, they hold to this day.

Often termed 'rice wine' in the West (a misnomer), sake or *nihonshu* – the name used since the post-war period, 'Japan sake' to distinguish it from Western-style alcoholic drinks – is made through a fermenting process using grain, somewhat akin to beer-making.

Key to the sake-making process are good *okome* (rice), good *mizu* (water) and the magical Aspergillus Oryzae. The latter is the dark greenish-yellow, fine powder *koji*, a fermenting agent that is added to steamed white rice, converting sugar to alcohol. This process from start to finish takes between one and two months, and the sake is ready to drink as soon as it drips from the barrel. It has an alcohol content of somewhere between 15% and 17%. Sake, unlike wine, does not have vintage years – its quality depends solely upon the conditions under which it is made; and foremost, the skill of the sake-maker. Nor is there the broad regional variation that affects wine – sakes can vary considerably from maker to maker.

SHINTO & SAKE

When walking aound shrines in Japan, it's hard not to notice the walls of sake barrels piled high; most renowned is the huge, colourful wall at Tokyo's Meiji Jingu. These barrels displayed out the front of Shintō shrines are called kazaridaru ('decoration barrels'), which are empty of liquid yet full of spiritual importance. Sake has long been a connection between Japanese people and the gods; at festivals and Shintō rites, people visit a shrine and will be given sake to drink in order to feel closer to the spiritual world. Sake brewers donate these sake barrels to shrines for ceremonies and festivals. Usually the smaller, local shrines will get their sake from a local brewer, but two main shrines – Meiji Jingu in Tokyo and Ise Jingu in Mie Prefecture – accept donations from every sake brewer in the country. There are also a few shrines that have actually been granted a licence to brew their own sake and, therefore, don't need to rely on donations at all.

Kyoto's Fushimi Inari-Taisha shrine, famous for its seemingly endless arcades of hundreds of bright vermillion torii (gates) climbing up the hillside, was dedicated to the gods of rice and sake by the Hata family in the 8th century. It's located a short way from the Fushimi Sake District, home to 37 breweries and one of the most famous sake-producing regions in the country.

TYPES OF SAKE

All sake is graded by the government into one of four categories: Chotokkyu, a kind of 'especially-special' class that is rarely available; Tokkyu special class; Ikkyu first class and Nikyu second class. However, these classifications are based in part on volume produced, not quality, so are of little value for the consumer.

Far more important for the layperson is the type of sake, and its *nihonshū-do* (classification of sweetness/dryness, based on a numerical scale: +20 indicating an extremely dry sake, -15 an ultra sweet one). The four main sake types are:

DAIGINJO

Top-of-the-heap, always a brewer's flagship sake. Made with rice milled so that 50% or less of the original size of the grains remains, it is always an intensely crafted, complex sake, and very expensive.

GINJO

Expensive, complex sake made with rice milled so 60% of the original grain remains. It is fermented at lower than average temperatures, using special yeast.

JUNMAI-SHU

Pure sake, made simply of rice, water, and *koji* without the addition of sugar, starch, or additional alcohol. No more than 70% of the rice grain remains after milling.

HONJOZO-SHU

Similar to *junmai-shu*, but with a small amount of alcohol purposefully added to enhance its fragrance.

Left: Sake at Tokyo's Meiji-jingū shrine
Below: Pouring sake at a ceremony

Local JIZAKE (LOCAL ARTISAN SAKE)

All are junmai-shu, unless otherwise indicated:

- **KASUMI TZURU, HYOGO PREFECTURE.** *Affordable, drinkable, smooth nigori-zake for the early spring.*
- **KUBOTA, NIIGATA PREFECTURE.** *Dry, good quality sake, popular in more upmarket izakaya.*
- **YOROKOBI GAIJIN, KAGAWA PREFECTURE.** *Slightly dry, slightly acidic junmai with above average alcohol content of 17% to 18%. Has many fans and just as many detractors.*
- **FUKUCHO NO HAKUBI, HIROSHIMA PREFECTURE.** *Unusual sparkling junmai nigori-zake made in rural inland Hiroshima.*
- **BIJOUBU, KOCHI.** *Junmai-shu 'mai', very crisp, semi-dry, fragrant, with the perfume of strawberries.*
- **KIKUIZUMI DENSHU, AOMORI PREFECTURE.** *Classy sake by Nishida Shuzo, a company dating back to 1878, from Aomori at the tip of the Tohoku region Northern Honshu.*
- **GUNMA IZUMI, GUNMA PREFECTURE.** *Characteristic, unpretentious sake, great value for money. Can be drunk warm.*
- **YOSHINOGAWA, NIIGATA PREFECTURE.** *The oldest sake brewery in Niigata Prefecture, one of Japan's top sake-producing regions.*
- **KOSHI-NO-KANBAI, NIIGATA PREFECTURE.** *Highly respected, one of Japan's best known sakes.*

The first two are generally reserved for special occasions, as their expense implies; the latter pair are for regular drinking. *Nama-zake* refers to sake that has not been pasteurised, and can fall into any of the classifications mentioned above. It needs to be drunk quickly once the bottle has been opened. *Nigori-zake* is a cloudy, unfiltered sake in which some of the lees have been allowed to remain. It is not a particularly delicate brew as the sweetness of the lees swamps out any delicacy in the sake, yet it is a popular late winter/early spring body-warmer. Its alcohol content is generally lower than other sakes.

163

HOW TO DRINK SAKE

Sake is generally drunk *hiya* (cold), when it is called *reishu*, *atsukan* (hot), or *nurukan* (warm).

Connoisseurs offer even finer classifications, including *hitohada* (lukewarm), *hanabie* ('flower-chilled' at 10°C), or *yukibie* (snow-chilled at 5°C). The finest sake is always drunk cold, the hot options are reserved for cold winter evenings when getting warm takes precedence over more aesthetic considerations. Either way, it will usually be served in a *tokkuri* (ceramic sake pot), with a small *ochoko* cup for drinking (reportedly derived from the Korean word 'chonku', meaning 'a small, shallow cup or dish').

It is polite to fill your drinking partner's glass first (usually the younger person fills the older person's glass), and then your partner in turn fills yours. However, by the end of a night's drinking, everyone has probably

© Jonathan Stokes/ Lonely Planet

Left: Sampling sake at Nihonshu Stand Moto *izakaya*; **Right:** It's polite to pour your partner's sake first

ditched convention in favour of *tejaku* (pouring your own).

Cold sake is also sometimes served in a wooden square open-topped box, or *masu*, thus it's known as *masu-zake*. The gentle pine aroma of the container mingles with the sake, which is often drunk across salt placed on the nearest corner of the *masu*, akin to a salted gimlet or margarita glass.

At rural inns, sake may be served hot in freshly cut hollow cylinders of green bamboo, which are placed in the ash of an *irori* (hearth) to heat. This gives the sake a pleasant bamboo aroma, and is known as *take-zake*.

A professional sake expert or *kikizakeshi* will judge a sake using a *kikijogo*, a small white *ochoko*, which has an appraisal mark (two concentric circles) imprinted in the bottom, for judging colour and clarity. The best colour is *aozae*, a slight yellow with a

tinge of blue. If sake has a brown shading, it most likely has too many sub-flavourings. A completely colourless sake will have a flat, two-dimensional flavour. Bouquet depends on a number of factors, and will indicate whether a sake is to be served by itself (as in the case of many very fragrant *daiginjo* sakes) or with food. As with a wine sommelier, a

kikizakeshi comes with an arsenal of specialist phrases with which to praise or damn the subject of his investigations. Some of the simpler terms are *amai* (sweet), *karai* (dry), *koku ga aru* (a phrase implying an earthy depth), *kuchi-atari* (a sake's initial impression or effect), and its opposite *kire* (the tail), and *okubukai* (suggesting deep-complexity).

© taka1022 / Shutterstock

165

Left: A cup of shōchū
Right: Japanese
wine is on the up

SHŌCHŪ

© takasuu / Getty Images

Although it probably originated in Okinawa, *shōchū* grain liquor is famously the drink of the southern island Kyushu. It also has a reputation as the heavy drinker's tipple of choice. This may be because until the end of the Edo period it was in general use as a medical disinfectant. Yet not all of it is rough, cheap firewater. The better versions are actually rather pleasant.

Shōchū is usually drunk cold, *rokku* (on-the-rocks) or as *shōchū oyuwari* (diluted with hot water). Oita prefecture produces *mugi-jochu*, distilled from

wheat, while Kagoshima prefecture prides itself on *shōchū* made from potatoes, *imo-jochu*. The Kochi Mutemuka sake brewery uses the pure waters of the Shimanto River to produce the unusual *kuri-jo-chu*, *shōchū* made from chestnuts. Unlike sake, this improves with ageing. However few *shōchū* drinkers seem to have the patience to keep a bottle for more than a few days. A very popular way of drinking it is in the cocktail called *chuu-hai* – *shōchū* mixed with flavoured soda and available canned and at izakaya and bars.

The southern tropical island of Okinawa produces its own version of *shōchū* called *awamori*, a powerful brew that the locals knock back like there was no to-morrow, usually accompanied by Okinawa Minyo folk singing and dance. It probably originated in Thailand (then Siam) and was brought to Okinawa during the Ryukyu Kingdom's 'Golden Age', during the 15th and 16th centuries. Even the origin of its name is a little mysterious, and no-one is sure whether the '*awa*' refers to the foam that is created during distillation, the foam generated during measuring for alcohol content, or the Foxtail-millet that it once contained. Serious connoisseurs search out *kusu*, *awamori* that has been aged for at least three years.

DRINKING AGE
The legal drinking age in Japan is 20. Bars generally don't require photo ID as proof of age, but nightclubs are required to check ID cards (of everyone, no matter how far past 20 you look).

BUDO—SHU: WINE

While Japan's vineyards are not yet threatening those of Bordeaux, Burgundy or the Barossa Valley, its reputation as a serious wine-producing country is on the rise and *budo-shu* (wine) is finally gaining the recognition it deserves. The most important of Japan's wine regions is Yamanashi, with a 1000-year history of grape growing; there are some very respectable tipples appearing on the scene, thanks to the country's unique *koshu* grape variety. Since 2010, *koshu* has been on the International Organisation of Vine and Wine (OIV) list of varieties, so it can be displayed on labels in Europe. These wines tend to have floral aromas and distinctive flavours, and are the perfect accompaniment to seafood, particularly a plate of fresh sashimi. One of the premier wineries in the Yamanashi region growing *koshu* grapes is the Katsunuma Winery. Established in 1885, family-owned Lumiere is one of the oldest wineries in Japan and uses natural farming techniques in its production of the *koshu* grape.

Other important wine-growing regions in Japan are the Yamagata Prefecture, known for its European varietals – Chardonnay and Merlot, as well as Delaware styles; Hokkaido's coastal city of Yoichi is known for its German grape varie-

AMAZAKE

At shrines, teahouses and winter festivals, you can sometimes find a sweet, nonalcoholic fermented rice drink called amazake, served hot.

ties and the famous Domaine Takahiko winery's pinot noir; and one of Japan's leading wineries, Chateau Mercian, in the Nagano Prefecture produces an award-winning Merlot.

UME–SHU PLUM WINE

Though not technically a wine, *ume-shu* is a popular drink in Japan which is also gaining popularity outside the country, too. It's actually a liqueur that is made from unripe ume (plum) fruit that is steeped in shōchū and sugar. It can be drunk straight, on the rocks or mixed with soda.

KAMPAI!

In Japan it's considered bad form to fill your own glass. Instead, fill the drained glasses around you and someone will quickly reciprocate; when they do, raise your glass slightly with two hands – a graceful way to receive anything. 'Cheers!' in Japanese is 'Kampai!'; glasses are raised though usually not clinked.

Left: Whisky may be served with ice or soda **Right:** Relaxing at an izakaya

WHISKY

Japan produces some of the finest whiskies in the world, from major makers Suntory and Nikka with their range of single-malts and blends, to cult-favourite small-batch producers such as Chichibu. Some favourite whiskies include the Yamazaki 12 from Suntory, which is light with dry spice notes and loads of fruity flavors; Nikka's Yoichi Single Malt with its subtle hint of smokiness; Suntory's Hibiki 17 blend; and the Akashi Single Malt from the White Oak Distillery.

If you find straight whisky curls your toes a little too much, try the popular Japanese highball, *haibō-ru*, instead. This refreshing summer cocktail is a mix of whisky and soda and can be found everywhere, including pre-mixed cans in *konbini* (convenience stores).

169

JAPAN'S REGIONAL CUISINE

Right: A tea ceremony with Club Ōkitsu, Kyoto

Left: A sushi board
in Tokyo

W hile the standard classics of *washoku* (traditional Japanese cuisine) can be found right across the country, Japanese food really comes alive in its unique regional variations. Japan's diverse landscape, from the tropical southern island of Okinawa through the lofty mountain ranges of the Japan Alps to the wintry highlands of its northernmost island of Hokkaidō, offers a bounty of different produce and ingredients to create an interesting mélange of regional cuisine.

Even the tiniest Japanese village has a *meibutsu* (a local speciality or dish) for which it is renowned. It is this specialisation that gives Japanese regional dishes their unique quality, rather than a major stylistic variation. However, one Japanese adage drily observes '*Meibutsu ni umai mono nashi*' – 'Lots of famous products, none of 'em any good'. It may be true that rampant commercialisation in heavily touristed spots has led to some dilution of quality, but – by and large – sampling the local speciality, with local vegetables, local rice and the local booze, is a fine way to travel the country. And it certainly will endear you to the people. The prefectural governments of the southwesternmost island of Kyūshū have even made this the mainstay of their island's economic development with their 'One village, one product' program.

HOKKAIDŌ

Japan's northernmost island, Hokkaidō is a fantastic place to eat, serving up specialities you won't find elsewhere in Japan – thanks to its bountiful land, ample coast and a climate that favours belly-warming dishes. Sapporo has the liveliest dining scene, while Niseko, with its star rising ever higher, is becoming more than just a ski spot – it's got some decent restaurants year-round.

Hokkaidō's best-known dish from the beloved *nabemono* (variety of hotpot dishes) is *Ishikari-nabe*. A wonderful winter hotpot, designed as sustenance via internal central-heating to fend off Hokkaidō's bitter cold winters, *Ishikari-nabe* is named for the small settlement near Sapporo that was once so dependent on *shake* (salmon) that it had its own 'Department of Salmon' in the town hall. No-one goes much to Ishikari, but the dish it gave birth to is found in just about every restaurant in Hokkaidō. It is satisfyingly simple, and very rich. Salmon is chopped and put into a heavy iron or earthenware *nabe* pot, and slowly cooked in Hokkaidō miso, with *jaga-imo* (potatoes), *hakusai* (Chinese cabbage), tofu, *negi* (leek), *daikon* (giant radish), *ninjin* (carrots), *konnyaku* (devil's tongue), kombu (seaweed), shitake or *maitake* mushrooms and mirin, seasoned with salt. That's the theory at least. In reality as long as there's salmon, miso and tofu, chefs seem to put in whatever they fancy.

Hokkaidō's fresh seafood is legendary, and topping its list is *shake*. Salmon is charcoal-grilled, steamed in sake, added to *zosui* rice soup, and indeed is served in any one of a thousand styles in the restaurants of Sapporo's foodtown, Susukino,

© Sean Pavone / Shutterstock

and in Hokkaidō-*ryōri* (specialist restaurants) throughout the country. Best of all, however, it appears in one dish we most certainly can thank the indigenous Ainu for, the sublime, unmissable, *ruibe*.

Ruibe is even simpler than *Ishikari-nabe*. Chefs take prime Hokkaidō *shake*, freeze it to -20°C or less, for more than twelve hours, slice it very thinly, and eat it dipped in the best *shōyu* (soy sauce). As the raw salmon melts in your mouth ('thaws' in your mouth?), the effect is magical. It may sound like a fish popsicle, but once you've experienced the sublime suffusion of salmon and soy sauce, you're hooked. And it may be simple, but that doesn't mean it isn't taken very seriously. Top Hokkaidō chefs won't slice it with knives, for fear of contaminating the *shake* with a metallic smell. Instead they use the sharp edge of an abalone shell.

AINU CUISINE

Hokkaidō's indigenous people, the Ainu, draw their ancestry back to the earliest settlers of Hokkaidō, while a distinct Ainu culture is believed to have emerged around 700 years ago. They were hunters, fishers and gatherers, settling along salmon runs and coastal plains. Following the formal annexation of Hokkaidō in 1869, the new Meiji government signed the Hokkaidō Former Aborigines Protection Act in 1899. Though well-meaning in name, it banned traditional practices, such as hunting and tattooing, along with the Ainu language.

It is a tragedy that little remains of Ainu cuisine. From 19th-century anthropological reports and travellers' diaries, we know that it made use of ingredients such as wild-caught salmon and deer, shoots and roots foraged from forests, seaweed, millet, bear fat and fish oil.

There are a handful of restaurants in Akan National Park that serve the few Ainu dishes that have survived, including ruibe; pocche *(traditional dumplings made from fermented potato mash); and* ohaw *(a soup of salmon or venison and wild vegetables).*

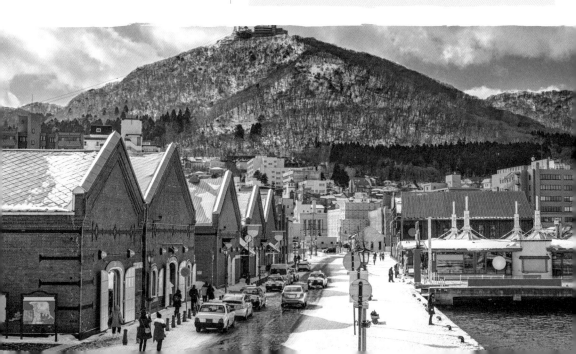

Hot on the heels of salmon in Hokkaidō cuisine is *kani* (crab), the great winter cold-water speciality, and for many Japanese, Hokkaidō is synonymous with crab. Winter is the season for *tarabagani* (king crab), *zuwaigani* (snow crab) and *kegani* (horse hair crab) from the frigid waters of the Sea of Okhotsk. The long-legged crabs of Wakkanai in the far north and Kushiro in the east are especially renowned, and are in season from December to April. Kushiro is also the *shishamo* (smelt) capital of Hokkaidō. Their season begins with Japanese railway-timetable precision on 10 October, but for the best fish, arrive in Kushiro a month later, when the fish are heavy with roe. Eat them broiled as an appetiser with sake.

Summer, meanwhile, is *uni* (sea urchin) season. The islands of Rebun-tō and Rishiri-tō are particularly famous for it. So is Shakotan, which means you can get good *uni* in season in southern and central Hokkaidō, too. Fish markets, sushi restaurants and *shokudō* serve *uni-don* (a bowl of rice topped with a mountain of fresh roe). Summer is also the season for the blooming red *hanasakigani* (spiny king crab), found only around Nemuro.

JINGISUKAN

This dish of charcoal-grilled mutton is the unofficial symbol of Hokkaidō, a legacy of the island's short-lived 19th-century sheep-rearing program. Its name – a Japanese rendering of Genghis Khan – comes from the unique shape of the cast-iron hotplate used to grill the meat, thought to resemble the warlord's helmet. The meat is grilled on the peak of the hotplate, allowing the juices to run down the sides to the onions and leeks sizzling on the brim. Jingisukan is served all over the island, though especially in the heartland of Sapporo, and is best accompanied by copious amounts of beer.

HOKKAIDŌ specialities

HAKODATE

Famed for its chemical-free butter made by nuns at the city's Trappist monastery, and *ika somen* – squid sliced so thinly as to resemble *somen* noodles, served with a raw quail's egg, *wakame* (seaweed) and *tsuyu* dipping sauce.

ASAHIKAWA

Its Ainu name means 'river where the waves are raging', and is best-known for crab, and for its original ramen. Asahikawa ramen features a soy-based broth, thin noodles and seafood, and has earned a reputation nationwide.

OBIHIRO

Located in the southeast of Hokkaidō, Obihiro is considered the breadbasket of Hokkaidō, lying as it does where the fertile Tokachi Plain is watered by the Tokachi-gawa river. In addition to being a main agricultural centre, it is famed for its sausages made at the government-sponsored Yachiyo-bokujo farm.

SAPPORO

The island's major city, the thriving, oft-freezing Sapporo, is where much of Hokkaidō's speciality products end up. Sapporo-ites are deeply proud of their miso-based Sapporo ramen, which is popular nationwide. Also try the wonderful *hime-masu* (trout) from nearby Shikotsu-ko lake.

TOHOKU

Left: Rowing past cherry blossom in Hirosaki Park, Hirosaki
Right: Preparing squid croquettes at Tsugaru Akatsuki Club, Aomori

The five prefectures that make up the Tohoku district— Aomori, Iwate, Akita, Yamagata and Fukushima — are very much *inaka* (the boondocks), and great hunting grounds for *inaka-ryōri* rustic cuisine.

AOMORI

Aomori is famous for its hotate- *ryōri scallop* cuisine, with the specimens from Mutsu-wan bay especially prized, and eaten as sashimi or in *nabemono*. Tohoku as a whole is partial to soups, not surprising considering the long, dark winters, and abundance of sea-fish and fresh vegetables. The fishers and farmers of Aomori thrive on *jappa-jiru* (cod soup with daikon seasoned with miso). In summer, *ichigoni* soup with *awabi* (abalone) and *uni* is served in the ryokan and *minshuku* (Japanese guesthouses) in and around Hachinohe city.

Wanko soba, an Iwate specialty, are cold buckwheat noodles, served in small bowls. The noodles are delivered at a fast and furious pace one after the other. You try to keep up, and finally signal your imminent explosion by covering up your dish.

In summer Morioka city specialises in a different kind of noodle –Morioka *reimen,* which are often served with Korean kimchee. The local dialect word for noodles is 'hatto' and they surface again in the local *udon-suki* dish *nambu hatto nabe* with seafood and vegetables.

The central part of the prefecture is renowned for its *kokuto-gyu*, black-haired beef, while Yuda Onsen hot spring prides itself on *suppon-ryōri*, cuisine featuring the soft-shelled turtles that are raised in its thermal waters.

AKITA

Akita produces some of the country's top quality rice, most notably *Akita-komachi*, and its sake is equally good, renowned for its characteristic depth and sweetness. *Shottsuru* soy sauce distilled from *hata-hata* sandfish or *iwashi* (sardines), thus somewhat akin to Thailand's Naam Plaa or Vietnam's Nuoc Mam, is considered Akita's unique *meibutsu* (though in truth it is actually made in one other Japanese location, on the Noto-hanto peninsula of Ishikawa where it is called *ishiru*). The prefectural dish is *kiritampo*: rice balls on skewers, cooked in a stew of vegetables, chicken and mushroom. Inaniwa town's Inaniwa udon noodles are also popular.

YAMAGATA

The brave folk of Yamagata combine fermented beans, *totoro-imo* (taro) and tofu to make the adventurous *natto-jiru* soup. A winter speciality soup of the Shonai region is *dongara-jiru* in which a whole cod is chopped into a stew of miso and salt. *Tama konnyaku* is devil's tongue stewed in a soy-sauce broth and served on skewers. Shonai is also a major producer of *kaki* (persimmons) and *sakuranbo* (cherries).

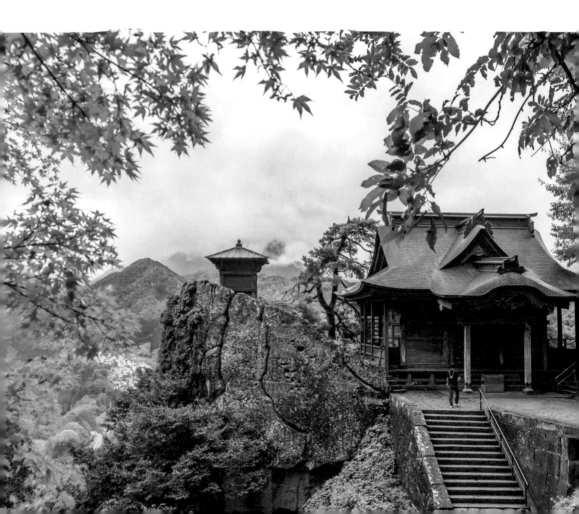

Clockwise from top: Boiling crab; *Kitakata ramen*; Funaoka Castle Ruins Park, near Sendai; Yamadera Temple, Yamagata

FUKISHIMA

Tohoku's southernmost prefecture Fukushima has a long, distinguished culinary pedigree, most noticeably the historic castle town of Aizu-Wakamatsu, with its sake and soba makers, and *tamari-joyu* (tamari soy sauce) producers. Today, however, it is probably best known for its *Kitakata ramen* made with thick, wavy *jukusei-men* noodles made in Kitakata. Its broth is a light *shōyu* and *tori-gara*, chicken broth mix. Mochi lovers will want to seek out *shingoro*: balls of glutinous rice mixed with *goma* (sesame) and *jaga-imo* (potatoes) and roasted *sumibiyaki*-style over a charcoal fire.

Autumn in Shinjuku-
gyoen, Tokyo

TOKYO

In truth, Tokyo has very few actual local specialities; its strength lies in its variety. You can get anything, and get it done to perfection: all the Japanese staples, such as tempura, *tonkatsu* (deep-fried pork cutlets), yakitori (chicken grilled on skewers), soba (buckwheat noodles) and *okonomiyaki* (savoury pancake); regional dishes from all over Japan, including Kyoto-style *kaiseki* (Japanese haute cuisine); and a wide spread of international cuisines.

But if there is one dish that Tokyo can truly claim, it's *nigiri-zushi*, the style of sushi most popular around the world today: those bite-sized slivers of seafood hand-pressed onto pedestals of rice. It's a dish that originated in the urban culture of Edo (the old name for Tokyo) and is sometimes still called 'Edo-mae' sushi (as in the style of Edo). A good sushi meal should be at the top of your Tokyo bucket list.

Two individual Tokyo-ites changed the course of sushi history. Matsumoto Yoshiichi in the 17th century introduced the use of rice vinegar into sushi rice to cut down on preparation time. The populace loved the new tart flavour. In the 1820s Sushi visionary Hanaya Yohei added raw fish to vinegared rice, which he served directly from his *sushi-yatai* (outdoor stall), and sushi as we know it today, from the Ginza to the West Coast, was born. Hanaya not only invented Edo-mae or *nigiri-zushi*, he also popularised the concept of fresh sushi served as quickly as possible, a concept that 130 years later Osaka-born conveyor-belt sushi-magnate Shiraishi Yoshiaki parlayed into a personal fortune. Yet it was not until 1923, when the Great Kanto earthquake leveled the city and rendered its surviving chefs unemployed that *nigiri-zushi* spread throughout Japan, as the skilled *itamae* (chefs) were forced to move in search of work.

TSUKIJI & TOYOSU

In 2018, Tokyo's central wholesale market moved from its famed Tsukiji location in Ginza to a new facility on the artificial island of Toyosu in Tokyo Bay, a fairly sterile structure clearly dreamed up by bureaucrats. The early-morning tuna auction and other parts of the market can be viewed by the public from glass-walled viewing platforms; entry to the market floor is limited to licensed buyers. The upper floors have some shops and restaurants, including sushi counters originally at Tsukiji.

At the heart of the original Tsukiji complex was the fish market, or *uogashi*. It began around the same time that Kyoto's Nishiki Market started to flourish; in the sixteenth century, when the mighty Shogun Tokugawa Ieyasu decreed that what the new capital really needed was fish. As most of its new occupants were carpenters who didn't know a herring from a handsaw (to paraphrase the Bard), he turned naturally to those inveterate gourmands, the good citizens of Osaka. Tokugawa invited the fishers of Tsukadajima village up to Edo with the promise of lucrative fishing monopolies if they would provide seafood for himself and the residents of Edo-jo castle. Soon

the neighbouring Nihonbashi Uogashi fish market was formed to pass the surplus on to the rapidly expanding population. The fish market boomed as wholesalers favoured by the Shogunate grew stinky and rich by bringing in fish from local ports, and selling it to market traders. Vegetable markets sprang up in the suburbs of Kanda, Kagome and Senju, modeled on the wholesaler-trader model of the fish markets, except that they also auctioned veggies directly to the public.

In the Meiji restoration, the wholesalers were stripped of their privileges, and the public auction system was instituted. When the city, and most of its markets, was levelled in the Great Kanto Earthquake of 1923, Tsukiji became fish-and-veg central.

Despite the move to its new location, there are many reasons to visit its old home. The tightly packed rows of vendors (which once formed the Outer Market) hawk market and culinary-related goods, such as dried fish, seaweed, kitchen knives, rubber boots and crockery. It's also a fantastic place to eat, with great street food and a huge concentration of small restaurants and cafes, most specialising in seafood.

TOKYO'S DINING DISTRICTS

Today's cosmopolitan madhouse that is Tokyo has magnificent restaurants of every persuasion on every street corner. That's not hyperbole, just plain fact. Even within the metropolitan mayhem, some areas retain their old specialisations.

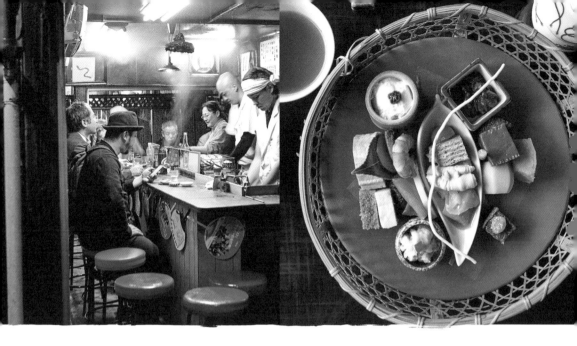

GINZA

This district is made up largely of upscale restaurants and great sushi restaurants. It can be an intimidating business walking into a Ginza sushi restaurant for the first time. Doubly scary if you sit at the counter and see a menu sans prices.

MARUNOUCHI & NIHOMBASHI

These neighbourhoods offer a load of midrange options for the local office crowd, particulary in Marunouchi, while classic Japanese can be found in Nihombashi.

ROPPONGI & AKASAKA

Both break-the-bank and midrange options are scattered around this area, with a good selection of international cuisines.

EBISU & MEGURO

This is where you'll find an abundance of cosmopolitan offerings, with excellent dining options in all price ranges.

SHIBUYA

Lively, inexpensive restaurants that cater to a young crowd, and some stylish, upmarket options on the fringes.

HARAJUKU & AOYAMA

Fashionable midrange restaurants and excellent lunch options aimed at shoppers.

SHINJUKU

High-end restaurants, under-the-tracks dives and everything in between. It's also a great neighbourhood for steaming bowls of ramen.

ODAIBA & TOKYO BAY

Family-friendly restaurants, mall food courts and chains in Odaiba; sushi with fish from the wholesale market in Toyosu.

ASAKUSA

Head here for unpretentious Japanese fare, old-school charm and modest prices.

From left: Kabuto, an izakaya on Shinjuku's Omoide Yokocho; A *hanakago* (flower basket) at Inshotei restaurant

SEEING STARS

Japan's capital holds the world record for the city with the highest number of Michelin-starred restaurants. The 2020 Tokyo edition of the Michelin guide included a whopping 226 starred restaurants, 11 of which were awarded three stars – the highest accolade.

© Ogasawara Hakushakute

KYOTO

Kyoto is one of the world's great food cities. In fact, when you consider atmosphere, service and quality, it's hard to think of a city where you get more bang for your dining buck. You can pretty much find a great dining option in any neighbourhood, but the majority of the best spots are clustered downtown.

© Sean Pavone / Shutterstock

Kyoto punches way above its weight in the culinary arena. Among the reasons for this is that Kyoto was the centre of the country for most of its history, and its chefs had to please the fussiest of palates in the realm: the imperial court, the nobility and the heads of the main religious sects.

Another reason for Kyoto's excellent cuisine is the surrounding natural resources. The city sits atop very good groundwater (essential for making good tofu, sake and tea), and has very fertile soil for growing vegetables in the city and surrounding areas. In fact, you can still find several distinct subspecies of vegetables in the city's markets known as *kyō-yasai* (Kyoto vegetables).

The result is a relatively small city packed with fine restaurants.

At the heart of all the cultured sophistication in Kyoto is the Gion district, with its geisha in all their powdered, deliberate, beauty; its exclusive ryotei restaurants, and its unforgiving mantra 'ichigen-san okotowari' – 'guests by introduction only...'. If you do manage to get beyond the doors of a top Kyoto restaurant, you'll find either the Zen-inspired, frugal and unadorned *cha-kaiseki*, or full restaurant-style (read

banquet) *kaiseki*. On the simplest level a *kaiseki* meal is made up of one soup and three side dishes, served with rice and pickles, yet often the courses run into double figures, their content determined by season and the whim of the *ryōri-cho* (top chef).

In the nation's collective imagination, Kyoto is temple-town, and indeed its vegetarian Buddhist-inspired cuisine is unmissable. Kyoto is famed for its tofu (soybean curd), a result of the city's excellent water and large population of (theoretically) vegetarian Buddhist monks. There are numerous *tofu-ya-san* (tofu makers) scattered throughout the city and a legion of exquisite *yudōfu* (tofu cooked in a pot) restaurants – many are concentrated in Northern Higashiyama along the roads around Nanzen-ji temple and in the Arashiyama area. One typical Kyoto tofu by-product is called *yuba* (sheets of the chewy, thin film that settles on the surface of vats of simmering soy milk). This turns up in many ryokan meals and *kaiseki* restaurants.

Yet Kyoto today is equally secular. It is a thriving university town, which might account for its unusually large concentration of ramen shops. There's no particular 'Kyoto style' although the

Clockwise from left: A
Kyoto fishmongers; Arashiyama
Bamboo Grove; Tofu at a Kyoto
ryokan; Jam Jar Lounge & Inn

dark, thick peppery broth of *shimpuku-saikan* is attracting much attention in ramen connoisseur circles.

If you have something of a sweet tooth, Kyoto will more than satisfy your cravings. *Wagashi* is a general name given to a variety of sweets and cakes that is available throughout Japan, and the traditional Kyoto confectionary is known as *kyo-gashi*. The city is the perfect spot to sample these sugary temptations, thanks to its long tradition rooted in tea ceremony and *wagashi* making.

GIFTS & SOUVENIRS

Gift-giving has a long history in Japan as a means of cementing business or familial relationships. As the year grows to a close people give oseibo gifts such as canned beer, and in summer ochugen gifts are exchanged: somen noodles and, again, beer are popular choices.

Similarly whenever a Japanese person travels domestically or abroad, they are duty-bound to bring back sackloads of omiyage or miyage-mono 'souvenirs' for company colleagues, family members, neighbours, the neighbours' dog, etc. The shopping list is inevitably huge, and more often than not the chosen gifts will be local meibutsu food-speciality products.

© Lauryn Ishak; Raymond Patrick; Ikunl / Shutterstock

KYOTO'S DINING DISTRICTS

Kyoto Station & South

There are places to eat scattered all around the Kyoto Station building and a handful of izakaya (Japanese pub-eateries) and local spots further south.

Downtown Kyoto

The centre of Kyoto's dining scene, it has the thickest concentration of restaurants in the city.

Southern Higashiyama

Offerings here fall into two categories: tourist establishments near the temples and refined places in Gion.

Arashiyama & Sagano

Cheap restuarants for tourists cram the main drag, with a few high-end spots further out and along the river with some lovely river views.

NISHIKI MARKET

Nationwide it is known as Kyo no daidokoro, Kyoto's kitchen, and a market has existed on the site of the city's Nishiki Market since the 17th century. Today over 100 stalls ply their wares in the covered, pedestrian-only arcade that stretches between Teramachi shōtengai (market streets) and Takakura-dōri in the heart of downtown Kyoto, and it is as much of a tourist attraction as the city's famed temples.

Japan's imperial family was long Nishiki's most prestigious and wealthy customer. Even today the Imperial Household, ensconced in the new upstart capital 500km east, orders its speciality foodstuffs from the market.

A stroll along Nishiki is a must for all Kyoto-bound food lovers. It is easy to spend several hours pottering, trying to fathom how to use many of the exotic wares on display. If you stop in at Aritsugu, knife-makers to the Imperial family for four centuries, it is also easy to spend your entire holiday budget.

FUSHIMI SAKE DISTRICT

Fushimi, home to 37 sake breweries, is one of Japan's most famous sake-producing regions. Its location on the Uji-gawa river made it perfect for sake production, as fresh, high-quality rice was readily available from the fields of neighbouring Shiga-ken and the final product could be easily loaded onto boats for export downriver to Osaka.

The largest of Fushimi's sake breweries is Gekkeikan Sake Ōkura Museum, the world's leading producer of sake. Although most of the sake is now made in Osaka, a limited amount is still handmade in a Meiji-era sakagura (sake brewery) in Fushimi. The museum is home to a collection of artefacts and memorabilia tracing the 350-year history of Gekkeikan and the sake-brewing process.

OSAKA

Japan's third largest city is as food-crazed as they come. Osaka's mercantile and sea-going heritage has long given it a rough-and-tough, no-nonsense image, and its industrious citizens have a reputation for partying as hard as they work. The saying goes that while Kyotoites will happily waste their fortunes on fine kimono, and Tokyoites on shoes, the Osakans have only one way to squander their riches – on food. There's even a word for it that has become Osaka's unofficial motto, *kuidaore*, the civilised practise of bankrupting oneself through sheer gluttony.

The city's love of good food is undeniable, from the entertainment districts of Umeda in the north to Shinsaibashi and Namba in the south. However real foodie heaven is Namba's gourmet-street, Dotombori-suji, and the neighbouring area of Sennichimae.

Dotombori's fame and fortune began with the success of its kabuki theatres, but soon the area began to teem with restaurants to service the Osaka revellers' culinary needs. Nearby Kuromon-ichiba market still provides the raw materials for the countless restaurants that line the Dotombori-gawa canal.

Crab-cuisine specialists Kani-Doraku and the ramen shop Kinryu with its fiery kimchee toppings and *shōyu* and pork-broth base have become nationally famous, yet for most Japanese, Osaka can only be synonymous with two dishes: *tako-yaki* and *okonomiyaki*. Yet contrary to the commonly held belief, Osaka cuisine is not all balls and mistranslated pizza. An abundance of quality ingredients from Osaka-wan Bay and the Seto-naikai Inland Sea, and the fertile plains surrounding the city, have meant that historically a sophisticated Osaka cuisine could evolve.

Clockwise from top: Aizuya is one of Osaka's top spots for *takoyaki*; *Okonomiyaki*; Cooking octopus balls

TAKOYAKI

It says something about Osaka's lack of pretension, when one of its best-known epicurean delights is 'octopus balls' or *tako-yaki*. These are tiny spherical wheat-flour pancakes to which diced octopus, shredded cabbage and other vegetables are added. They are often grilled in front of the customer at outdoor food stalls, and come topped with *katsuobushi*, bonito flakes, and a 'secret' sauce of the owner's own invention. They are cheap, filling, fattening and forever associated with Osaka. Needless to say, this does nothing to lessen their popularity, not least for a midnight stop-off between izakaya and karaoke-den. Take care when biting into one: they are known to burn the roof of your mouth off.

OKONOMIYAKI

Okonomiyaki is perennially (and inaccurately) translated as 'a kind of Japanese pizza'. It is nothing of the sort. It's a discus-sized savoury pancake of wheat-flour, egg and water topped with your *konomi* – 'whatever takes your fancy'. Usually this means meat, squid, vegetables and finely-chopped cabbage. Restaurant proprietors cook it in front of you on a flat hotplate and serve it with sweet brown sauce or mayonnaise, often garnished with dried and powdered *aonori* (seaweed), or *katsuobushi* flakes that 'dance' as they heat up. Osakans can't get enough of the stuff, yet few know (or at least care to admit) that it was almost certainly invented in either Kyoto or Tokyo.

It actually came to Osaka from Tokyo after WWII, when it immediately proved a massive hit. The Osaka gourmands increased the variety of ingredients, added the sweet topping sauce and began serving it at a counter where the guest could sit and watch the *okonomiyaki* being made. This cheery informal style of serving an inexpensive, tasty meal suited the Osakans to a tee, and the rest is, as they say, history.

KAITEN—SUSHI

Osaka is home to one more culinary claim-to-fame, thanks to its favourite son Shiraishi Yoshiaki who opened the nation's first *kaiten-sushi* restaurant, Genroku-zushi, in Higashi-Osaka in the 1950s. This Osaka invention goes by many names in English: conveyor-belt sushi, sushi-go-round or sushi train. It's all the same – plates of sushi that run past you along a belt built into the counter (you can also order off the menu).

OKONOMIYAKI

There are around 2000 okonomiyaki restaurants in Hiroshima, specialising in Hiroshima-yaki, which adds noodles to the Osaka version. Typical varieties are nikutama-soba with pork, eggs and ramen noodles (don't let the name mislead you into thinking it is buckwheat), or nikutama-udon with udon noodles, although other types include squid and even, yes, oysters. The best place to explore is the Okonomimura, or 'Okonomi village' complex in central Hiroshima, which has 25 restaurants under one roof.

© voy ager / Shutterstock

Left: A belt-load of sushi
Right: The 'floating gate' of Itsukushima Shrine, Hiroshima

HiROSHiMA PREFECTURE

Hiroshima has an excellent range of Japanese and international eating options for all budgets, especially west of Peace Memorial Park and south of the Hon-dōri covered arcade. Many restaurants offer good-value set-lunch menus, and mall basements are budget-friendly. Hiroshima is famous for oysters and *Hiroshima-yaki* (noodle- and meat-layered *okonomiyaki*). Other regional specialities in this prefecture include:

Miyajima specialises in *anago* (conger eel) caught along the Miyajima shoreline.

Fukuyama city, and the nearby port of Tomonoura, have been renowned for their *tai-ryōri* (sea-bream) cuisine for nearly four centuries, and throughout May the *tai-ami* matsuri festival (fishing for sea bream with nets) takes place.

Innoshima has *suigun-nabe,* 'navy hotpot', as its speciality. It features fish, shellfish, and seaweed, and was traditionally eaten by members of the Murakami fleet before going into battle to give them courage and ensure victory.

Hiroshima prefecture too has its own regional ramen speciality, *Onomichi-ramen*, a *gyukotsu/tonkotsu* (beef/pork) broth-based ramen from the town of the same name.

Saijo is the best place to sample the prefecture's sake during its annual Sake Tasting Festival each October.

SHiKOKU

Shikoku is a foodie's paradise and the Kagawa Prefecture in the northeast of the island is known throughout Japan for *Sanuki-udon*, the local noodle dish, with square-shaped, thick, wheat-flour noodles. You'll find them everywhere. As Shikoku is an island, exquisite seafood is widely available, too. Try the vegetarian *shōjin-ryōri* (devotion cuisine) that is served to pilgrims at temple lodging houses – half the fun is trying to identify what the ingredients are.

TOKUSHIMA

Fertile valleys and a long coastline make Tokushima a land of fresh food. Noodles are popular, with Tokushima city home to over 100 shops offering 'Tokushima ramen'; Handa sōmen (thin wheat-flour noodles) have been produced here for over 250 years. Sweet potatoes and *renkon* (lotus root) are grown around Naruto, while wakame (seaweed) is harvested from the sea.

Tokushima prefecture's **Naruto** is famous for its whirlpools and its wakame seaweed. The former bash the latter around adding thickness and texture until the seaweed is perfect for making *dashi* stock.

The inland **Iya** region, famed for its scarily wobbly straw bridge Kazura-bashi crossing the *ayu*-filled Iyagawa river, specialises in Iya soba – plain, handmade buckwheat noodles that border on the rough-hewn.

Donari town offers *tarai* udon – thick noodles served in a large bowl and eaten with fish broth, while **Handa** produces the excellent, thin summer noodles Handa *somen*.

KAGAWA

Sanuki-udon truly is everywhere here. This Kagawa favourite is available on almost every corner. *Iriko-meshi* is a popular sardine and rice dish, while rice crackers are made from shrimp caught in the Inland Sea. Grilled chicken on the bone is also considered a local speciality, as is top-class olive-fed beef.

Kagawa prefecture, once known as Sanuki, doesn't get enough rainfall for full-scale rice-production, so it relies heavily on wheat. Thus its *meibutsu* is *Sanuki-udon.* Reputedly brought from Seian in China by Buddhist saint Kobo-daishi in the 9th century, this tasty udon is most popular in **Takamatsu** city.

Shōyu-mame eaten throughout the prefecture except on Shodoshima island are parched broad beans soaked in locally made soy sauce containing sugar, and red pepper is added to this sauce.

Other popular dishes include *manba-no-kenchan, leaf-mustard fried with tofu,* and seasoned with *shōyu* and *oshinuki-zushi* prepared with small inland sea fish, served with Sanuki-mai locally grown rice.

KŌCHI

With its long Pacific coastline, Kōchi Prefecture is known for its seafood, particularly *katsuo-tataki*, seared bonito fish that is thinly sliced and eaten with grated ginger. *Sawachi-ryōri* is a huge plate (a *sawachi*) of seafood, with various varieties of both sashimi and sushi.

Left: *Mikan* orchards in Ehime Prefecture
Right: Bonito is cooked over the grill

Kochi is synonymous with the exquisite *katsuo-no-tataki bonito fish* lightly braised over a charcoal grill, raw in the centre, served sliced as sashimi in a light vinegar and shōyu sauce.

Its *shiokara* (salted offal) is especially prized, and is nicknamed *shutou* ('sake theft') because it accompanies the drink so perfectly that sake-less gastronomes are forced to turn to crime.

The rest of Japan knows Kochi for its celebratory cuisine *Sawachi-ryōri* in which local vegetables and seafood, *nimono*, *agemono*, and fruits are piled extravagantly on one large platter – the *sawachi*. However it is so prohibitively expensive that it is rarely eaten outside the big tourist hotels.

On the coastline look for **Niitaka** *nashi Asian pears*, each individually wrapped while still on the tree!

Last but not least **Monobe, Kitagawa**, and **Umaji-mura** produce the marvellous yuzu citron, a main ingredient in ponzu dipping sauce.

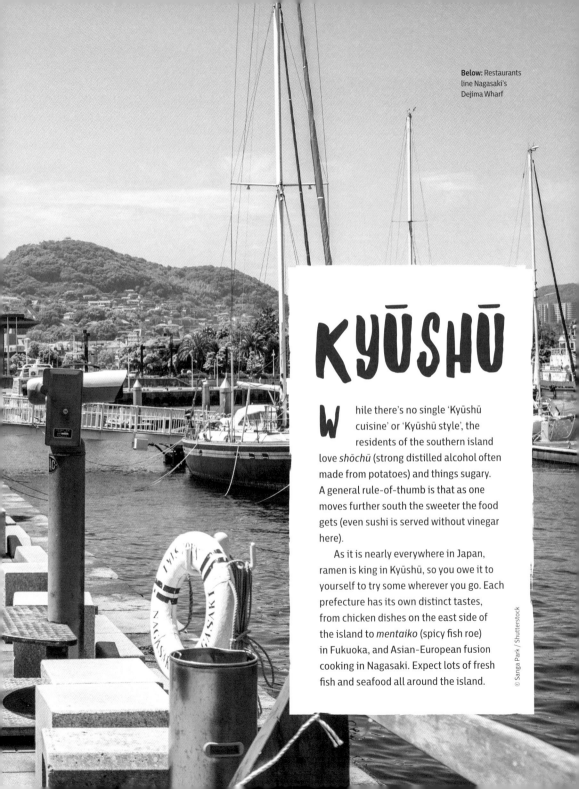

Below: Restaurants line Nagasaki's Dejima Wharf

KYŪSHŪ

While there's no single 'Kyūshū cuisine' or 'Kyūshū style', the residents of the southern island love *shōchū* (strong distilled alcohol often made from potatoes) and things sugary. A general rule-of-thumb is that as one moves further south the sweeter the food gets (even sushi is served without vinegar here).

As it is nearly everywhere in Japan, ramen is king in Kyūshū, so you owe it to yourself to try some wherever you go. Each prefecture has its own distinct tastes, from chicken dishes on the east side of the island to *mentaiko* (spicy fish roe) in Fukuoka, and Asian-European fusion cooking in Nagasaki. Expect lots of fresh fish and seafood all around the island.

KYŪSHŪ'S SPECIALITIES

Some of Kyūshū's other best-known dishes include...

Fugu-ryōri
Fukuoka-ites love this blowfish served as finely sliced sashimi, or in *zosui* (rice soup).

Hakata Ramen
For the rest of the country, Fukuoka means but one thing, Hakata Ramen. The city lends its name to the strong white *tonkotsu* pork-broth ramen that is found on every street in the city, and nowhere is it more popular than at Fukuoka's famed outdoor street stalls.

Kani (Crab)
Saga, Japan's smallest prefecture, is home to excellent crab cuisine using the *gazami* or *takesaki-kani* crab from the Ariake-kai sea.

Nagasaki Champon
Nagasaki's best-known dish owes its existence to a homesick overseas Chinese merchant from Fujian who created this stew of seafood, vegetables and pork in a thick ramen broth, most famously served in Nagasaki's Chinatown.

Uni-meshi
Serious gourmands head to Iki-jima off the coast towards Fukuoka for the exquisite (and elsewhere cripplingly pricey) *uni-meshi*, plain white rice cooked with sea-urchin and *shōyu*.

Satsuma-age
Kyūshū's southernmost prefecture, the idiosyncratic Kagoshima was once the fiefdom of the Satsuma clan, and that name often occurs in its regional speciality foods. Best known is *Satsuma-age*, where fresh fish are ground into a paste, flavoured with local sake, and deep fried.

Onsen-tamago
Hot-spring festooned Oita Prefecture uses its thermal waters to make *onsen-tamago* (spa-boiled eggs) most notably in the port of Beppu.

OKINAWA

The food of Okinawa shares little in common with that of mainland Japan. Technically part of the Kyūshū region, it was merely a century ago that the Ryukyu kingdom was incorporated into the country, and the southern islands still have a strong sense of being caught between those two behemoth cultures of China and Japan.

Local dishes to try include *umibudō* (sea grapes – a type of seaweed), *mimigā* (sliced pigs' ears marinated in vinegar) and *gōyā champurū* (stir-fry containing bitter melon, an Okinawan vegetable). While travelling through the Southwest Islands, be sure to sample the local firewater, *awamori*, which is distilled from rice and has an alcohol content of 30% to 60%.

Clockwise from left: Kabira Bay, Ishigaki-jima; Dish of *kare raisu*; Performers at the Tanadui festival, Taketomi-Jima

© Matt Munro / Lonely Planet

The OKINAWAN DIET & LONGEVITY

According to the United Nations, Japan has the largest number of people aged 100 and over in the world. Okinawans have a 40% greater chance of living to 100 than other Japanese people. Traditionally, Okinawan longevity rates have been the highest in Japan, in part thanks to the 'Okinawan diet', which focuses on whole foods, plant-based protein, a good percentage of green and yellow vegetables, and not shunning carbohydrates – sweet potato being one of the main staples. Their long life and good health might also be attributed to a physically active lifestyle (working predominantly in agriculture and fishing up to an older age) and possibly just good genes.

© Matt Munro / Lonely Planet

© Matt Munro / Lonely Planet

OKINAWAN SPECIALITIES

The humble pig: Every part of the animal is used, from top to bottom. On a hot summer night, pigs ears washed down with cold Orion beer are irresistible.

Rafte: Very similar to the mainland *buta-no-kakuni* is pork stewed with ginger, brown sugar, soy sauce and *awamori* until it almost falls apart.

Inamudo'chi: Okinawa's celebratory dish, is also known as *inoshishi-modoki* ('fake wild-boar soup'), and consists of pork, *kamaboko* (processed seafood), shiitake mushrooms and *konnyaku* in a bonito-fish/pork broth mixed with *shiro-miso*.

Ikasumi-jiru: A stamina-inducing soup of pork stewed in squid ink.

Irabu-jiru: Another dish designed to pick you up in the enervating heat of an Okinawa summer is the enticing *irabu-jiru* (sea-snake soup). Dried sea-snake is stewed for several hours with *konbu* and pork.

Okinawa-soba: Don't let the name fool you, it isn't buckwheat noodles, but rather udon, served in a pork broth. Okinawa does make buckwheat noodles, which are called *udunyama-soba*.

Hiraya-chi: A Okinawan 'crepe' containing *nira* (chives) which was once the staple dish when people were trapped in their house during typhoons.

Left: A lantern hangs in a restaurant entrance in Okinawa

PHRASES EATING OUT

breakfast
朝食/朝ごはん
chō·sho·ku/a·sa·go·han

lunch
昼食/昼ごはん
chū·sho·ku/hi·ru·go·han

dinner
夕食/晩ごはん
yū·sho·ku/ban·go·han

snack
間食/スナック
kan·sho·ku/su·nak·ku

to eat
食べます
ta·be·mas

to drink
飲みます
no·mi·mas

I'd like … …
をください。
… o·ku·da·sai

I'm starving!
お腹がすいた。
o·na·ka ga su·i·ta

FINDING A PLACE TO EAT

Can you recommend a cafe?
どこかいいカフェを知って
いますか?
*do·ko ka ī ka·fe o shit·te
i·mas ka*

Can you recommend a restaurant?
どこかいいレストランを
知っていますか?
*do·ko ka ī res·to·ran o
shit·te i·mas ka*

Where would you go for a cheap meal?
安い食事をするなら
どこに行きいますか?
*ya·su·i sho·ku·ji o su·ru
na·ra do·ko ni i·ki·mas ka*

Where would you go for local specialities?
名物を食べるなら
どこに 行きますか?
*mē·bu·tsu o ta·be·ru na·ra
do·ko ni i·ki·mas ka*

Where would you go for a celebration?
お祝いをするならどこに
行きいますか?
*oy·wai o su·ru na·ra do·ko ni
i·ki·mas ka*

I'd like to reserve a table for one person/two people.
1人/2人の予約を
お願いします。
*hi·to·ri/fu·ta·ri no yo·ya·ku o
o·ne·gai shi·mas*

I'd like to reserve a table for (eight) o'clock.
(8)時の予約を
お願いします。
*(ha·chi)·ji no yo·ya·ku o
o·ne·gai shi·mas*

Are you still serving food?
まだ食事が
できますか?
*ma·da sho·ku·ji ga
de·ki·mas ka*

How long is the wait?
どのくらい待ちますか?
do·no ku·rai ma·chi·mas ka

AT THE RESTAURANT

When you book for more than three, you'll always be seated at a table. When you make a booking for two or less, make sure you request a table if you don't want to end up at the counter. You can say 'at a table, please': tē·bu·ru de o·ne·gai shi·mas.

I'd like a table for (five), please.
(5)人分のテーブルを
お願いします。
*(go)·nim·bun no tē·bu·ru o
o·ne·gai shi·mas*
For five, please.

5名です。
go mē des

I'd like nonsmoking, please.
禁煙席をお願いします。
*kin·en·se·ki o o·ne·gai
shi·mas*

I'd like smoking, please.
喫煙席をお願い
します。
*ki·tsu·en·se·ki o o·ne·gai
shi·mas*

I'd like …, please.
…をお願いします。
… o o·ne·gai shi·mas

the menu (in English)
(英語の)
メニュー
*(ē·go no)
me·nyū*

a children's menu
子供の
メニュー
ko·do·mo no me·nyū

the drink list
飲み物の
メニュー
no·mi·mo·no no me·nyū

a half portion
半人前
han·nim·ma·e

What would you recommend?
なにがお勧めですか?
na·ni ga o·su·su·me des ka

What's in that dish?
あの料理に何が入って
いますか?
*a·no ryō·ri ni na·ni ga hait·te
i·mas ka*

Can you tell me what

traditional foods I should try?
伝統的な食べ物は
どんなものがおすすめ
ですか?
*den·tō·te·ki na ta·be·mo·no
wa don·na mo·no ga
o·su·su·me des ka*

I'll have that.
あれをください。
a·re o ku·da·sai

Please decide for me.
おまかせします。
o·ma·ka·se shi·mas

Does it take long to prepare?
料理に時間がかかりますか?
*ryō·ri ni ji·kan ga
ka·ka·ri·mas ka*

Is service included in the bill?
サービス料込みですか?
sā·bis·ryō ko·mi des ka

Are these complimentary?
これはただですか?
ko·re wa ta·da des ka

I'd like (the chicken).
(鶏肉)をお願いします。
*(to·ri·ni·ku) o o·ne·gai
shi·mas*

I'd like a local speciality.
地元の名物を
お願いします。
*ji·mo·to no mē·bu·tsu o
o·ne·gai shi·mas*

Please bring …
…をください。
… o ku·da·sai

a knife/fork
ナイフ/フォーク
nai·fu/fō·ku

a glass
グラス

gu·ra·su

a serviette
ナプキン
na·pu·kin

a spoon
スプーン
spūn

a wineglass
ワイングラス
wain·gu·ra·su

I'd like it …
…ください。
… ku·da·sai

boiled (in hot water)
ゆでて
yu·de·te

boiled (in stock)
煮て
ni·te

deep fried
揚げて
a·ge·te

fried
炒めて
i·ta·me·te

grilled
グリルして
gu·ri·ru shi·te

medium
ミディアムに
して
mi·dya·mu ni shi·te

rare
レアにして
rair ni shi·te

re-heated
温めなお
して
a·ta·ta·me·now· shi·te

steamed
蒸して

mu·shi·te

well done

ウェルダンに

して

we·ru·dan ni shi·te

with the dressing on the side

ドレッシングを

別にして

*do·res·shin·gu o be·tsu ni
shi·te*

I don't want it deep fried.

揚げないでください。

a·ge·nai·de ku·da·sai

I don't want it fried.

炒めないでください。

i·ta·me·nai·de ku·da·sai

I don't want it re-heated.

温めなおさないで

ください。

*a·ta·ta·me·now·sa·nai·de
ku·da·sai*

I'd like it with …

…を付けてお願いします。

*… o tsu·ke·te o·ne·gai
shi·mas*

I'd like it without …

…を抜きでお願いします。

… o nu·ki de o·ne·gai shi·mas

chilli

唐辛子

tō·ga·ra·shi

garlic

ニンニク

nin·ni·ku

ginger

ショウガ

shō·ga

sauce

ソース

sō·su

seaweed

のり

no·ri

soy sauce

しょう油

shō·yu

horseradish

わさび

wa·sa·bi

COMPLIMENTS & COMPLAINTS

Bon appetit! (lit: I receive)

いただきます

i·ta·da·ki·mas

I love this dish.

この料理が大好きです。

ko·no ryō·ri ga dai·su·ki des

I love the local cuisine.

地元料理が大好きです。

*ji·mo·to·ryō·ri ga dai·su·ki
des*

That was delicious!

おいしかった。

oy·shi·kat·ta

It was a real feast.

ごちそうさま

go·chi·sō·sa·ma

I'm full.

お腹がいっぱいです。

o·na·ka ga ip·pai des

This is cold.

これは冷たいです

ko·re wa tsu·me·tai des

This is spicy.

これはスパイシーです

ko·re wa spai·shī des

This is superb.

これは素晴らしいです

ko·re wa su·ba·ra·shī des

PAYING THE BILL

I'd like the bill, please.

お勘定をください

o·kan·jō o ku·da·sai

There's a mistake in the bill.

請求書に間違いが

あります。

*sē·kyū·sho ni ma·chi·gai ga
a·ri·mas*

NONALCOHOLIC DRINKS

sparkling mineral water

炭酸ミネラルウォーター

tan·san·mi·ne·ra·ru·wō·tā

still mineral water

炭酸なしのミネラル

ウォーター

*tan·san·na·shi
no·mi·ne·ra·ru· wō·tā*

hot water

お湯

o·yu

lemonade

レモネード

re·mo·nē·do

LOOKING FOR

appetisers

前菜

zen·sai

soups

スープ

sū·pu

entrees

アントレー

an·to·rē

salads

サラダ
sa · ra · da
main courses
メインコース
mēn · kō · su
desserts
デザート
de · zā · to
à la carte
一品料理
ip · pin · ryō · ri
drinks
飲み物
no · mi · mo · no
milk
ミルク
mi · ru · ku
orange juice
オレンジジュース
o · ren · ji · jū · su
soft drink
ソフトドリンク
so · fu · to · do · rin · ku
water
水
mi · zu
(cup of) tea …
…紅茶(1杯)
… kō · cha (ip · pai)
(cup of) coffee …
…コーヒー(1杯)
… kō · hī (ip · pai)
with (milk)
(ミルク)入り
(mi · ru · ku) · i · ri
without (sugar)
(砂糖)なし
(sa · tō) · na · shi
… coffee
…コーヒー
… kō · hī

black
ブラック
bu · rak · ku
iced
アイス
ai · su
strong
濃い
koy
weak
薄い
u · su · i
white
ホワイト
ho · wai · to
Japanese green tea
お茶
o · cha
barley tea
麦茶
mu · gi · cha
green leaf tea
煎茶
sen · cha
oolong tea
ウーロン茶
ū · ron · cha
powdered green tea
抹茶
mat · cha
roasted rice tea
玄米茶
gem · mai · chai
roasted tea
焙じ茶
hō · ji · cha
cappucino
カプチーノ
ka · pu · chī · no
decaffeinated
デカフェ

de · ka · fe
espresso
エスプレッソ
es · pres · so
latte
カフェラテ
ka · fe · ra · te

ALCOHOLIC DRINKS

beer
ビール
bī · ru
brandy
ブランデー
bu · ran · dē
champagne
シャンペン
sham · pen
chilled sake
冷酒
rē · shu
cocktail
カクテル
ka · ku · te · ru
plum wine
梅酒
u · me · shu
sake
酒
sa · ke
shochu highball
酎ハイ
chū · hai
shochu spirit
焼酎
shō · chū
warm sake
お燗
o · kan
a shot of rum

ラムをワンショット
ra·mu o wan·shot·to
a shot of vodka
ウォッカをワンショット
wok·ka o wan·shot·to
a shot of whisky
ウィスキーをワンショット
wis·kī o wan·shot·to
a bottle of … wine…
ワインをボトルで
… wain o bo·to·ru de
a glass of … wine …
ワインをグラスで
… wain o gu·ra·su de
dessert
デザート
de·zā·to
red
赤
a·ka
rosé
ロゼ
ro·ze
sparkling
スパークリング
spā·ku·rin·gu
white
白
shi·ro
a … of beer
ビールを…で
bī·ru o … de
glass
グラス
gu·ra·su
jug
ジャグ
ja·gu
large bottle
大ビン
ō·bin

large mug
大ジョッキ
dai·jok·ki
small bottle
中ビン
chū·bin

IN THE BAR

When going out, keep in mind that some bars impose a 'table charge' (tē·bu·ru·chā·ji テーブルチャージ). At the bar, if you fancy a bite with your drinks, check out which bar snacks (o·tsu·ma·mi おつまみ) are on offer.

Excuse me.
すみません。
su·mi·ma·sen
I'm next.
次は私です。
tsu·gi wa wa·ta·shi des
Q: What would you like?
何を飲みますか?
na·ni o no·mi·mas ka
U: I'll have …
…をお願いします。
… o o·ne·gai shi·mas
Same again, please.
同じのをお願いします。
o·na·ji no o o·ne·gai shi·mas
No ice, thanks.
氷なしでお願い
します。
kō·ri·na·shi de o·ne·gai shi·mas
I'll buy you a drink.
1杯おごります。
ip·pai o o·go·ri·mas
It's my round next.

次は私の番です。
tsu·gi wa wa·ta·shi no ban des
Do you serve meals here?
食事はできますか?
sho·ku·ji wa de·ki·mas ka
How much is the table charge?
テーブルチャージはいくらですか?
tē·bu·ru·chā·ji wa i·ku·ra des ka

DRINKING UP

Cheers!
乾杯!
kam·pai
This is hitting the spot.
お腹に染みます。
o·na·ka ni shi·mi·mas
I feel fantastic!
気分がいいです。
ki·bun ga ī des
I think I've had one too many.
ちょっと飲みすぎました。
chot·to no·mi·su·gi·mash·ta
I'm feeling drunk.
酔いました。
yoy·mash·ta
I'm tired. I'd better go home.
疲れました。
うちに帰ります。
tsu·ka·re·mash·ta
u·chi ni ka·e·ri·mas
Can you call a taxi for me?
タクシーを呼んで
くれますか?
tak·shī o yon·de ku·re·mas ka

VEGETARIAN & SPECIAL MEALS

SPECIAL DIETS & ALLERGIES

Halal and kosher food might be hard to come by, even in the big smoke, but you might want to try your luck with these phrases.

Is there a halal restaurant?

イスラム教徒のための
ハラルレストランは
ありますか?

*i·su·ra·mu·kyō·to no ta·me
no ha·ra·ru res·to·ran wa
a·ri·mas ka*

Is there a kosher restaurant?

ユダヤ教徒のための
コーシャーレストラン
はありますか?

*yu·da·ya·kyō·to no ta·me no
kō·shā res·to·ran wa
a·ri·mas ka*

Is there a vegetarian restaurant?

ベジタリアンレストランは
ありますか?

*be·ji·ta·ri·an res·to·ran wa
a·ri·mas ka*

I'm on a special diet.

私は特殊な
食餌制限をしています。

*wa·ta·shi wa to·ku·shu na
sho·ku·ji·sē·gen o shi·te
i·mas*

I'm a vegan.

私は厳格な
菜食主義者です。

wa·ta·shi wa gen·ka·ku na

sai·sho·ku·shu·gi·sha des

I'm a vegetarian.

私はベジタリアンです。

*wa·ta·shi wa be·ji·ta·ri·an
des*

I'm allergic to …

私は…にアレルギーが
あります。

*wa·ta·shi wa … ni a·re·ru·gī
ga a·ri·mas*

dairy produce

乳製品

nyū·sē·hin

eggs

卵

ta·ma·go

gelatine

ゼラチン

ze·ra·chin

gluten

グルテン

gu·ru·ten

honey

蜂蜜

ha·chi·mi·tsu

MSG

グルタミン
酸ソーダ

*gu·ru·ta·min·
san·sō·da*

nuts

ナッツ類

nat·tsu·ru·i

peanuts

ピーナッツ

pī·nat·tsu

seafood 海産物

kai·sam·bu·tsu

ORDERING FOOD

I don't eat …

…は食べません。

… wa ta·be·ma·sen

Could you prepare a meal without …?

…抜きの料理をお願い
できますか?

*… nu·ki no ryō·ri o o·ne·gai
de·ki·mas ka*

butter

バター

ba·tā

eggs

卵

ta·ma·go

fish

魚

sa·ka·na

fish stock

魚のだし

sa·ka·na no da·shi

meat stock

肉のだし

ni·ku no da·shi

oil

油

a·bu·ra

pork

豚肉

bu·ta·ni·ku

poultry

鳥肉

to·ri·ni·ku

red meat

赤身の肉

a·ka·mi no ni·ku

INDEX

NOTES

Published in May 2021 by Lonely Planet
Global Limited CRN 554153
www.lonelyplanet.com
ISBN 978 18386 9051 9
© Lonely Planet 2021
10 9 8 7 6 5 4 3 2 1
Printed in Malaysia

Written by: Paula Hardy
Managing Director, Publishing: Piers Pickard
Associate Publisher: Robin Barton
Editors: Jessica Cole, Carly Hall, Karyn Noble, Nora Rawn, James Smart
Art Direction: Daniel Di Paolo
Layout Designer: Kerry Rubenstein
Cover illustration: © Muti, Folio Art
Spot illustrations: Louise Sheeren, Tina García
Print Production: Nigel Longuet

Lonely Planet offices

USA
230 Franklin Road, Building 2B, Franklin, TN 37064
T: 615-988-9713

IRELAND
Digital Depot, Roe Lane (off Thomas St),
Digital Hub, Dublin 8, D08 TCV4

STAY IN TOUCH lonelyplanet.com/contact